THE SCENT OF A CRIME

THE
SCENT OF
A CRIME

RON STEPHENSON

NEW
HOLLAND

*To the families of the victims of these crimes
and the police officers killed in the course of their duty*

First published in Australia in 2004 by
New Holland Publishers (Australia) Pty Ltd
Sydney • Auckland • London • Cape Town

14 Aquatic Drive Frenchs Forest NSW 2086 Australia
218 Lake Road Northcote Auckland New Zealand
86 Edgware Road London W2 2EA United Kingdom
80 McKenzie Street Cape Town 8001 South Africa

National Library of Australia Cataloguing-in-Publication Data:

Stephenson, Ron.
The scent of a crime

ISBN 1 74110 170 0.

1. Crime - Australia. 2. Criminal investigation -
Australia. I. Title.

364.994

Publishing Manager: Robynne Millward
Project Editor: Glenda Downing
Designer: Karlman Roper
Production Manager: Linda Bottari
Printed in Australia by Griffin Press, Adelaide

10 9 8 7 6 5 4 3 2

Roll of honour photographs courtesy of the Australian Police Journal,
all other photographs Ron Stephenson (except cover).

CONTENTS

INTRODUCTION

Over half a century ago, as a 19-year-old youth, I decided to join the NSW Police Force. I had completed an engineering apprenticeship, played plenty of sport and was a member of the Cronulla Surf Life Saving Club. I felt that I possessed the personal qualifications to make that step. With a clean record and having proudly established that I met the physical requirements, I was admitted to the force on 13 August 1951.

I remember very clearly the words of the uniformed sergeant as I arrived at Regent Street Police Station in Sydney to begin my first day with the NSW Police Force. The sergeant's name was Bill Howard and he flatly said to me, 'Welcome, son. But I tell you, it's a bad time. The job's stuffed.'

I found the work adventurous and rewarding. Things were new to me—modern, today. Bill Howard had seen many changes during his 30 years of policing, probably hoping all the time that everything would remain as it was when he had joined the job. But they didn't. Times had changed.

A few years later, I was rostered to work night shift in a detective's patrol car. The officer I reported to that night was Detective Senior Sergeant Herb North, who held an elite position known then as the Reception Officer at the Criminal Investigation Branch.

'Sarge,' I said to Herb North at one point. 'Have you seen much change in the job since you joined?'

Herb looked at me for a moment. 'Son,' he muttered. 'I joined the job as a police cadet at the age of seventeen. I worked in an office filing wireless messages, answering the phone and doing general office duties. Thirty years later, I'm doing the same thing. The only thing that's changed is that now I'm doing bloody night work.'

One aspect of policing that definitely never changed throughout Herb's career, or Bill Howard's, or mine, was the danger. For any police officer, whatever the role, the presence of danger is always near. A police officer never knows when he or she may suddenly be called upon to face a perilous situation. And police are human—they are conventionally educated men and women who wish to follow a career in law enforcement. Some are young, some not so young.

Throughout my career, I discovered that many aspects of the job did change. However, it remained always an adventure and I, like so many of my colleagues, kept a strong desire to rid the streets of crooks and help those in need. I wanted, too, to progress through the ranks from constable to more senior positions where something I said or did meant more. I soon learned, however, that such promotions did not come without responsibility and accountability.

During my early years on the job, in the 1950s, public feeling railed against police officers who, at least part of the population felt, represented a cold 'authority'. We didn't like it, but perhaps this feeling was created by the way we stood aloof from the community. That was the philosophy we were taught in those days—don't become too friendly with the public, they may later ask for favours. Always give the appearance of self-assurance, as this is the way to control most situations. Look the part, though only through bitter experience will you ever become the part.

I served under nine police commissioners. Each one had a different management style, and the performance of the force could generally be equated to the style of that leader. The last of the nine was John Avery, who was sworn in as commissioner in 1983.

John Avery's leadership style was one of working with the community and he introduced a program that is known today as 'community-based policing'. Community consultancy committees were formed, staffed by responsible citizens who worked with their local police. Neighbourhood Watch was implemented, another scheme to bring the public closer to their police. A Safety House initiative was introduced, where approved homes displayed a sign indicating that the occupants were able to offer children protection and comfort in the event of an emergency.

Each of these enterprises gave the community greater respect for police culture. To me, it seemed the public were becoming more familiar with the daily problems facing police officers and in some parts of the community a feeling of empathy began to replace resentment. In other parts, though, animosity still lingered just below the surface, waiting for a chance to come to life.

On a Christmas Day in the late 1980s, as Detective Superintendent in Charge of Operations at the Criminal Investigations Branch, I sent two homicide investigators to the outskirts of Ivanhoe, a town in the far west of New South Wales. A body had been found in bushland, obviously the victim of foul play. These two detectives couldn't have been happy, but they left their homes and family with no complaint over the severe interruption to their festivities. This was their job. They lived for many of the ensuing days in a tent, preserving the crime scene, making investigations and examinations.

Investigating a murder is inevitably a painful experience. For those not familiar with policing, I'll quickly summarise what this procedure involves.

Homicide investigators and their junior colleagues will head to the crime scene, which, if not already 'secured', soon will be. 'Contamination'—property disturbed because the wrong people have been allowed access and moved or even stolen exhibits—could be a disaster. Arrangements are quickly made for crime scene officers to expertly and professionally examine the area, to take photographs and gather exhibits. The local coroner may attend to make his or her observations of the site. Identification of the body has to be established, then comes the unenviable task of notifying the next of kin.

Following a comprehensive inquiry at the crime scene, including interviews with any witnesses, the body is removed to the local morgue, escorted by a police officer who arranges admission. This officer provides details of the death to the pathologist who will perform the post-mortem. The officer remains at that autopsy, making a record of any wounds or injuries detected. In remote districts, the officer might be asked to physically assist in this examination by passing the tools and holding and labelling parts of the body. All details of the homicide investigation are recorded. Once this was done on typed pages called a running sheet. Nowadays the records are computerised.

Homicide investigations, as for all types of crime, might be short, or many long hours could be needed as part of a protracted inquiry. Whatever the length of time, in every homicide case, a brief of evidence is prepared by police for the information of the coroner. After an arrest has been made, the offender is escorted to the crime area in what is called in police parlance 'the run around'. Evidence is gained about the events leading up to the crime and what occurred afterwards.

For everyone involved, the court process is always arduous. Most accused persons claim their right to defend the charge against them and have the prosecution prove their case. The matter is heard in two court sittings. The first is called the committal proceedings and is held at the lower court—Coroner's Court or Local Court—before a magistrate who, if he or she considers a prima facie case has been established, will commit the accused to stand trial. This trial is held in the Supreme Court before a judge and a panel of 12 jurors. The verdict is in the hands of that jury. If a guilty verdict is returned, the judge will hand down the sentence.

Forty of my happiest years were being part of the so-called 'police culture', meeting and mixing with men and women who were totally dedicated to policing and putting the welfare of others before their own.

The job has changed, but it's not stuffed. One major change is that of accelerated promotion. In my days on the force, a certain number of years had to be served on each rank and a qualifying examination completed successfully before officers became eligible for promotion to the next. This guaranteed experience as well as efficiency. That system has been abolished and younger officers can apply for a higher position, whatever their age.

I learned my trade on the streets and in the gutters of Sydney as an operational police officer. I tagged along with the old, hard-nosed, experienced cops, listening and learning in practical, real-life lessons.

Scientific and technical aids have advanced since my retirement as a police officer in 1991. DNA testing, laser fingerprint examinations, computer databases and information technology are all now available to assist the investigator. The results, however, will always depend on the expertise of the person doing the investigation. He or she is the matrix. Everything flows from him. He has to make the decision, not the machine.

I will always remember a case where police were investigating the death of a young woman from a drug overdose. She was separated from her husband and lived alone in a suburban cottage. The detective, when examining the interior of the house, noticed the toilet seat was in the up position. Strange, he thought. Females don't usually lift the seat. His curiosity aroused, he looked more closely into the would-be suicide. The result was the arrest and conviction for murder of the estranged husband and a male accomplice who had given the victim a forcible 'hot shot' of narcotics. The accomplice had lifted the seat when he used the toilet. Human curiosity, not a machine, solved that crime.

Introduction

When researching the information relating to the stories in this book, I was amazed to find that so much had been lost in the transfer of hard copy material onto computer. I was pleased that I was a 'hoarder' and had kept copies of my investigations in order to accurately recount the facts.

In revisiting these crime stories, I have relived my 40 years of policing, bringing back memories, some good and some rotten. They were all solved 'the old way', using intuition, suspicion, doggedness and the odd informant.

An old, street-hardened senior detective once said to me at a crime scene, 'Let's have a sniff around here.'

The scent of a crime is compelling.

CHAPTER ONE
YOUNG COURAGE

'Blessings on your young courage boy...For that is the way to the stars.'

Virgil

The birth of two baby boys in 1963 could be described as fate for the two young lives that began that year, hundreds of kilometres apart, but which would come together with tragic results 26 years later.

Allan Wayne McQueen was born in Lismore, New South Wales. At a young age he moved with his parents John and Shirley, sister Carole and brother Barry to Ballina and later to Coffs Harbour. Allan learned his trade as a carpenter, holding down extra jobs as a doorman at local nightclubs and as a general cleaner. He was not afraid of work.

His uncle, Athol McQueen, a Kyogle farmer and champion boxer, represented Australia at the 1964 Olympic Games in Tokyo. Athol gained the distinction of having knocked down Joe Frazier (who later became heavyweight champion of the world) when they fought as amateurs. Allan followed his uncle's practice of training daily and became more than handy with his hands. He remained undefeated after nine amateur bouts.

Allan soon expanded to surf club membership at Coffs Harbour, where he associated with fellow club members who were police officers. Through this association came the desire to become a policeman. Allan had developed a strong physique and earned the nickname of 'Big Al'.

The young McQueen was 24 years old when, after two unsuccessful attempts to join the NSW Police Force, he was finally accepted as a police trainee. He studied hard and with diligence, and in his final examinations he came fourth in his class of 194 recruits.

Allan Wayne McQueen was now a cop.

On 27 June 1987, the young police officer started work as a probationary constable at the Sydney Police District. This district contained some of the true trouble spots of Sydney—Kings Cross where the nightclubs and strip joints thrived; Redfern and Waterloo with their large Aboriginal population; Sydney Harbour and the wharf area; The Rocks, a tourist haven where pickpockets and con men flourished; and the central business district of Australia's largest city, where anything could, and usually did, happen.

Initially, Allan lived in the western suburbs of Sydney, but having spent the last few years near the surf, he yearned to get back to the beach. So when a fellow police officer, Steve Tedder, offered shared accommodation with him in a flat at surfside Manly, a northern Sydney beach suburb, Allan jumped at it. He joined Tedder at the Manly Surf Life

Saving Club and quickly offered to help the club's chief instructor with the training of new members.

First of all, Big Al wanted to be a good cop. He hoped to later obtain a transfer to his 'real home', the far north coast of New South Wales. He didn't own a car, so would ride his bicycle to Manly Wharf, then travel by ferry to Circular Quay chatting endlessly with the deck crew. He would then ride from the Quay to the Sydney Police Centre at Surry Hills. He was a chronic worker and would arrive at work hours before he was rostered to commence duty.

There was little wonder that he soon transferred into the Sydney District Anti-Theft Unit, where he would work in plainclothes, training to become a detective. Every reason existed for the ever-present smile on his handsome face. He loved being a policeman and enjoyed the life that he was leading.

Monday 24 April 1989 was a typical autumn day in Sydney. Sunny, with a hint of coolness on the early light northerly breeze. The start of another working week, but a short one—the following day was Anzac Day, a public holiday, a day when all Australians remember their war dead and those who survived the many conflicts since Gallipoli, so many years earlier. Sadly this Anzac Day eve would affect the lives and memories of many people. Monday was also a day that Allan McQueen worked a rostered day off, filling in for a work mate who had an urgent commitment.

John Albert Edward Porter was born in Brisbane, Queensland, on 26 June 1963, the second child in a family of five. Porter's father, Kenneth, had been born in the United Kingdom, migrated to Australia and worked in

Queensland as a builder's labourer. He married May Olive Porter, an Aboriginal woman. Kenneth Porter came from a family with a strong military background, and was authoritarian, sometimes violent, in his approach to his family.

May Porter left her husband and moved to Western Australia when John was only 10 years old. The boy was receiving little formal education. When his father died five years later, May returned to Brisbane. Her son was sent to Boys' Town, which was conducted by the De La Salle Catholic Brothers. There John obtained his Junior School Certificate. He was then 16, and promptly left school to explore the country. He hitchhiked around western Queensland, New South Wales and Victoria, working as a railway fettler, fruit picker, spare parts salesman and general hotel hand, staying only a short time at each job

Living such an itinerate lifestyle got John into trouble. He was only young and had had little family life or supervision of any description. Before a Children's Court, and still aged only 16, John Porter was sentenced to an indefinite period of confinement for breaking and entering, stealing, and stealing a motor vehicle.

From this time on, whether in custody or free, Porter did plenty of physical training. He developed into a strong young man, 190 centimetres tall and weighing in around 90 kilograms. The young Koori also developed a quick, strong temper. Maybe it was a result of his turbulent upbringing. He dealt with most problem situations by using his fists, adopting a 'tough guy' attitude.

The juvenile institutions that were supposed to help could not alter Porter's character. His childhood years had determined his future.

In 1981, Porter turned 18. In the eyes of the legal world he was now an adult. He 'graduated' to adult prisons, spending most of his early manhood in custody. A naive man who underestimated his own propensity for violence, he compiled a history of offences in jail—'using threatening language', 'disobeying lawful orders', 'causing damage to property' and 'assaulting prison officers'.

On the few occasions when Porter was not in jail, his lifestyle was aimless. He lived in hostels and halfway houses. In such places it is almost impossible not to associate with people who have a criminal background. John Porter had no chance of living anything but a life of crime.

In the Corrective Services system, Porter gained an 'A2' classification—he was high risk. While serving a sentence in Grafton Jail, he iron-barred another prisoner and assaulted a prison officer, breaking the officer's teeth and splitting his tongue.

During a short period of release from jail in August 1984, while on parole, Porter armed himself with a shortened shotgun, a hammer and a mask, and held up staff at the Commonwealth Bank at Ashfield, in the west of Sydney, and escaped with over $12,000. He was arrested and subsequently returned to prison, this time with a 15-year sentence. He served only five years of that jail term, being released from Sydney's Parklea Prison on 3 April 1989. John Albert Porter was now 26 years old and had lived with violence all his life.

THE SHOOTING

Jason Donnolley was a probationary police constable, 19 years of age, with 10 months' experience as a NSW Police officer. He was stationed at Central Police Station, a patrol of the Sydney Police District.

During a police officer's period of probation, he or she gains knowledge of how the entire police force operates by spending a week at a time with Traffic Section, a detective squad and other units. On 19 April 1989, Jason Donnolley was seconded to work for seven days with the Sydney District Anti-Theft Unit.

The Anti-Theft Unit was made up of 15 officers, dressed casually, specialising in street patrol, ever alert for the shoplifter, car thief or criminals consorting with each other. Working with the unit was Ross Kenneth Judd, a more experienced police officer. Judd was 25 years of age and held the rank of Constable lst Class, a 'one striper'. On 24 April 1989, Judd was rostered as a member of a three-man team, with Constable Allan McQueen and the new trainee, Probationary Constable Jason Donnolley. They were to work an 8am to 4pm shift, patrolling the inner city of Sydney.

John Porter was also considering doing an inner-city patrol, but for an entirely different reason. Released from jail only five weeks, he already had in his possession a .32 calibre pistol and a large amount of ammunition. His plans for 24 April were to steal a car and commit an armed hold-up. Porter was on parole until 1995, but crime was the only thing he knew how to do. He felt more at ease with a firearm on his body and a knife strapped to each leg.

Porter left a small fibro house in Marrickville in Sydney's inner west about 9am, conspicuous by his hairstyle of long dreadlocks. Dressed in a grey, army-style jacket, grey trousers and blue jogging shoes, only he knew that the slight bulge in the left-hand pocket of his jacket was the .32 calibre Browning hand gun. He caught a train to the city, alighted at Museum Station and walked through Hyde Park towards St Mary's Cathedral. There was an extensive street parking area around the cathedral, with two-hour parking meters. Porter knew, as did the drivers of the cars, that the elapsed time showing on the meter was a good indication of when the owner might be expected to return.

At 11.30pm, 24 April 1989, Ross Judd, Allan McQueen and Jason Donnolley cruised through the central business district of Sydney heading towards St Mary's Cathedral. Judd was the driver, Allan McQueen was seated beside him in the front seat with Donnolley perched in the rear. Each was armed with a departmental firearm: a .38 calibre Smith and Wesson six-shot revolver.

The police car slid into Haig Avenue behind the cathedral. The parking spaces were all occupied. A man with a Bob Marley-style hairdo was taking a more than casual interest in a white Cortina sedan. He tried the handle of the driver's door before he spotted the police car coming slowly towards him.

Allan McQueen and Jason Donnolley left the car, with Ross Judd remaining close to the car radio. John Porter, his heart pounding, had retreated into Phillip Park and attempted to hide behind a large fig tree.

'Just a minute. What are you doing here?' called McQueen as he walked towards the nervous Porter.

'Just waiting for a mate,' came the uninspiring reply.

'We're police. Would you mind turning your pockets out?' asked McQueen.

John Porter's mind was working in overdrive. Here were three cops intending to search him and he knew that when they found the gun, he was going back to prison for at least six years, the remaining period of his parole. He did what he knew best. With a solid, unexpected punch, he knocked Allan McQueen to the ground, produced the pistol and rapidly discharged three bullets, two of them hitting the police officer.

Allan didn't feel the bullets enter his body as he lay on the ground. The first one ripped into his left arm, spinning him around like a top. The second punctured his back. The third shot passed through the left side of Donnolley's body.

The wounded officers drew their service revolvers and fired at the fleeing Porter. McQueen scrambled to his feet and, driven by instinct, ran after the offender. Porter was racing along Haig Avenue, shooting back at the police. Donnolley stumbled after the offender but was soon halted by his injury.

Ross Judd, in the car, had seen the attack on his work mates and the exchange of gunfire. Allan McQueen was now bleeding profusely from the chest and blood had sprayed up his neck and along his arms. Judd and Donnolley pushed McQueen into the front seat of the police car. McQueen, in shock, was staring at the roof of the vehicle and gasping for air.

Judd shouted into the police radio handset, 'A20! Officers down in Haig Avenue! Am en route to Sydney Hospital!'

POLICE RESPONSE

The police radio barked that unforgettable message across my office at the Police Centre at 11.36am. Detective Chief Inspector Kevin Parsons also heard the call and we both drove to the scene of the shooting.

'Repeat. Two officers down. Suspect is six feet two, olive complexion, solid build, long grey trousers and jacket, brown hair in dreadlocks,' boomed out of every city police car.

'Jesus, who's been shot?' I demanded of a startled young policeman at the crime scene who, only minutes before, had been unloading barriers from a police truck to be used in crowd control at tomorrow's Anzac Day march.

'Two blokes from the Anti-Theft Unit. One doesn't look too good,' he replied.

The crime scene was sealed off and Kevin Parsons left for the hospital. I was a superintendent and remained at the scene and directed operations. The planning of a major operation was automatic after so many years. Specialists from Ballistics, Scientific, Fingerprints, Photogrammetry and Crime Scene units were called to my command post. A team of detectives was assembled at the Sydney Police Centre to interview witnesses.

The stark facts were evident. Constable Allan McQueen lay in a Sydney hospital in a critical condition, Constable Donnolley was in the same hospital in a serious condition, and the man who shot them had escaped.

THE SEARCH

After the shooting, Porter fled the city, catching a taxi to Glebe. He had no money and offered the cabby his watch. Sensing trouble, the driver was pleased to see the back of his passenger.

John Porter composed himself and realised that the cab driver would soon become aware of who his fare had been. A clash with police was not new for him, but this certainly was the most serious trouble he had ever brought upon himself. He went to the home of a friend, a hairdresser who cut off his dreadlocks, immediately transforming Porter's appearance.

He was driven by his friend to 193 Sydenham Road, Marrickville, the home of David Gundy, another friend. There he remained until dark, before boarding an interstate train on his way to Brisbane. By 8pm that night, Porter was safely out of Sydney.

I left the scene of the shootings mid afternoon and returned to my office. The police investigation had to be given a codename. The crime had been committed at the intersection of Haig Avenue and Boomerang Street, so we settled on the codename Operation Haig..

A description of the offender together with a photofit composite photo were prepared and distributed to the media. The offender's appearance was distinctive because of his unusual hairstyle and it was hoped that with a display of the photo on TV news outlets, an identification might be made.

Kevin Parsons walked into my office and the expression on his face told me that he had grim news: Allan McQueen was in a bad way.

'He's in Ward Sixteen and a leading specialist is looking after him. He's lost a kidney and part of his liver and most of one lung. Jason Donnolley's been admitted too, but thank God he's going to be alright.'

'Did you see Allan McQueen?' I asked.

'Yes. He was lying on a bed and all I could do was hold his hand,' Kevin said sadly.

Shortly after the broadcasting of the photofit during the news bulletins, the switchboard lit up like cracker night. I never had much faith in these type of photo images, they all looked the same to me. I was about to change my mind.

Four prison warders contacted police, separately, each with identical information. The man depicted in the photofit was John Albert Porter. Each officer had regular contact with him at Parklea Prison before his recent release. A parole officer from Enmore also rang, certain that Porter was the wanted man. Porter was his parolee, but had failed to report for over a week.

A police car was dispatched to the Criminal History Section at Parramatta to gather prison photos and records of Porter. By 7.30pm, I had them all on my desk.

I was astounded when I read Porter's criminal history. 'This bastard's not due out of jail for another six years,' I exclaimed to Kevin Parsons.

'He's out though, and more dangerous than ever,' came his reply.

Ross Judd and Jason Donnolley both 'put their finger' on the photo of Porter. Within eight hours of the shootings, the offender, hitherto unknown, had been positively identified. But it was one thing to know who you were looking for and another to find him.

THE NEXT DAY

Anzac Day dawned and a meeting took place in the Homicide Squad office at the Police Centre. Jackie Renshaw was a drug addict and prostituted herself to support her habit. Jackie was looking for police assistance with a couple of warrants for non-payment of some small fines, hoping that the warrants would be withheld until she was able to pay them. She knew Porter and gave the investigators recent photographs taken of the wanted man. He was dressed in a singlet, and the tattoos on both arms gave great identifying features. Porter was sitting on a multi-coloured, striped lounge inside premises at 193 Sydenham Road, Marrickville. Surveillance was placed on the home and police were ready if Porter showed himself.

Steve Tedder had remained at the bedside of Allan McQueen since the shooting. The wounded officer had regained consciousness after surgery. Tedder asked his flat-mate what happened.

'We saw this bloke near the cars and he was trying the doors. I went up to him with Jason and showed him my ID. I started to search him and he had a single key. He dropped it and king hit me,' said McQueen through the pain barrier that still remained, despite the sedatives.

'Did he hit Jason too?' asked Tedder.

'I don't know. I tackled him and tried to get the cuffs on him. There were two bangs and I rolled away. Then he fired again. I chased him and fired three shots. I thought I got him,' replied McQueen.

'Oh, you're a lucky boy, mate,' said Tedder, trying to reassure his friend. 'With that big chest I'm surprised they didn't bounce off.'

'It will take more than two bullets to stop me,' came the reply. Allan McQueen was trying hard to raise a smile.

'Do everything the good nurse tells you, okay? I'll let you rest,' said Tedder as he stood up to leave for the first time since the shooting. 'I'll see you soon.'

With a squeeze of his mate's hand, Detective Steve Tedder left the bedside of his best friend, not knowing that he would never again see Big Al alive.

The usual 'gigs', or police informants, came forward with bits of information about Porter's whereabouts. One known as 'Tony' described the offender as crazy. He had been in touch with Porter since the shootings and had seen the gun and ammunition still in his possession. According to Tony, Porter carried the bullets in a woollen sock and was prepared for World War III. He would never be taken alive by police.

THE RAID

A decision was made to make a forced, surprise raid on the premises at 193 Sydenham Road, Marrickville. Operational plans were drawn up and an eight-man team of officers from Special Weapons Operations Squad (SWOS) were selected as the entry team.

The crew would be led by Sergeant Jim Brazel. Jim was an imposing man—six feet plus tall and built like a battering ram. His piercing, deep brown eyes were set in a balding, suntanned head. Jim had dealt with emergency entries for a decade and faced the wrong end of a firearm on countless occasions. He was a fitness fanatic, training hard five days of the week—an ideal leader.

At 5.30am on 27 April 1989, Brazel led his team to the vicinity of the targeted address. The premises had been converted from a small butcher's shop into a suburban residence. The lock on the front door had been identified as the prime entry point which would be broken by the 'keyman' with a sledge hammer.

Six officers were each armed with a Remington 870, pump-action firearm, capable of being fired from the shoulder or from ready for action position. They had a .729 inch diameter barrel and could be used in many roles including chemical agent delivery, and were fitted with a torch on the barrel to assist in night vision. Even though the shotgun was a powerful weapon, it was considered the safest for use in building entry due to lack of penetration of shot through walls and doors. There was no doubt that this weapon held a distinctive psychological advantage over offenders.

The sledge hammer hit the door at 5.55am and the SWOS entry team, dressed in their black combat clothing, moved with precision timing into the darkened building. Loud calls of 'Police! Police!' alerted the occupants of their arrival.

A man stirred from his sleep on a sofa, but was quickly controlled. He was not John Porter. Detective Sergeant Terry Dawson moved towards a bedroom with the torch on his shotgun beaming onto the partly open door. With a quick movement of his foot, he kicked the door fully open and entered the room shouting 'Police! Police!'

A male voice returned the greeting with 'You cunts, you cunts.' The man, dressed only in his underpants, had jumped from his bed and grabbed the barrel of Dawson's shotgun.

'Don't!' screamed Dawson. 'We're police. Don't.'

'Fuck off,' the man answered, and with a solid wrench of the firearm, against the grip held by Dawson, the weapon discharged.

The pellets from the shell raced up the man's left arm, blowing his wristwatch into a wall, where it remained embedded. Several of the slugs deflected from the watch into his chest and he dropped to the floor.

A light was turned on. The wounded man was not John Porter.

First-aid treatment was given by the police, before an ambulance raced the victim to nearby Prince Alfred Hospital. He was identified as David Gundy. He was also Aboriginal.

From later information we learned that Gundy was born in Casino in northern New South Wales on 17 June 1959. He was christened Antoniou Baden Polliette and known by his friends as Tony. As a teenager, he took the name of David John Gundy after the name of a deceased relative. Gundy's upbringing was poor. He lived with his family in a tent on the banks of the Richmond River at Casino. He rarely went to school and was eventually made a ward of the state, living with a variety of foster parents. He gained several minor criminal convictions.

When Gundy turned 18, his term as state ward was over. He became friendly with an Aboriginal girl named Doreen (Dolly) Eatts and they lived together in a de facto relationship for three years. In 1979, they fostered a baby boy named Bradley. Gundy stayed in regular employment up until the time of his shooting.

At 7am on the morning of the police raid, news was brought to me from the hospital that Gundy had not survived the shooting.

At the time of the raid at Marrickville there was no sign of Porter. Other occupants of the house were Richard McDonald, Marc Valentine and David Gundy's son Bradley. 'Dolly' Eatts, Gundy's wife, was absent. Information began to emerge. On 2 April 1989, John Porter met his old friend Richard McDonald at the Paradise Club, a strip joint in Kings Cross. Over the next three weeks, he visited his friend at Sydenham Road on a number of occasions.

McDonald told police, 'It was on the 20th April. He just said out of the blue, "I don't know whether to show you this or not." He pulled out a pistol from his waistband and said, "What do you think of this?" He pulled out a sock full of bullets and said if you drill down the centre of the bullet, put mercury in it and seal it with wax, you've got a hollow point. He was fucking mad.'

When McDonald saw the photofit image of the suspect for the police shootings on the television news, he realised that it was of his friend Porter. However, he did nothing about it.

Observations made by police at Gundy's home showed the multi-coloured, striped lounge on which Porter had been photographed. A bankcard in the name of Porter was also located. The raid, however, was 24 hours too late to arrest the offender.

I now had a double task: to continue the search for John Porter and organise an investigation into the shooting of David Gundy.

The media had a field day—police had killed an Aborigine. The headlines shouted: 'Aboriginal Legal Services Threatens Charges Over Gundy Death', 'Sixty Seconds from Door to Death', 'SWOS in Action—Bang,

Crash: Send Us the Bill', 'Kind Family Man Shot in Cold Blood', 'Police Kill Wrong Man in Raid Bungle', 'Police Boasted Fugitive Would Be Blown Away'.

The situation was so inflamed that the State Coroner, Mr Kevin Waller, called a preliminary hearing of the required inquest to introduce a sense of order in the matter and reduce the atmosphere of near hysteria which seemed to pervade the death of David John Gundy.

THE SEARCH MOVES INTERSTATE

Another gig came forward with a lettergram he had received from Porter which contained just a single telephone number: 268-2737. The gig rang the number, preceded by the STD code 07. A male voice answered and said, 'John'.

'What are you doing?' asked the gig. 'Why didn't you tell me that it was you who shot the two police officers?'

'I didn't want you to panic knowing what happened,' came the reply.

'Do you know who died? Your friend Gundy,' the informant told him.

'Bullshit,' exclaimed Porter. 'Is that the house they raided? I must have been given up. I'm going.'

A check of the phone number showed that it was connected to 48 Nudgee Road, Hamilton, in Queensland, the home of relations of the wanted man. A raid on the premises by Queensland Police proved to be too late. Porter had again escaped.

Kay Lynette Rowley was a 47-year-old married woman who lived with her family in the Gold Coast suburb of

Sorrento. At 3pm on 3 May 1989, she had just completed her shopping in the tourist resort of Southport. She hurried to her car in the parking area at the rear of the shops. Mrs Rowley was due to pick up her two children from school and the time was getting along.

She paid little attention to the tall, dark, well-built man standing alongside a battered 1972 Holden sedan parked adjacent to her own vehicle. The man was dressed in black clothing—shirt, trousers and jacket. Even his felt cowboy hat was black.

Mrs Rowley got into her car and, as she did, the tall man moved. He roughly pushed the woman across the front seat and slid in behind the driver's wheel.

'Don't be frightened. Do you know who I am?' he growled at the terrified woman.

'No,' came her startled reply.

'I'm John Albert Porter. I'm wanted by the police. I shot two cops in Sydney. I've got to get to Sydney because they know I'm up here. You look like a nice lady and you've got a nice car. Don't worry. I won't hurt you. Don't scream,' said Porter.

Kay Rowley summed up the man pretty quickly. He was obviously desperate. She had never before heard anyone recite their full name, but then she was unfamiliar with the manner in which prison inmates addressed the authorities, always with their complete name. Any doubt she had about the man's desperation was quickly dispelled when he produced a hand gun from inside his jacket.

'I want you to drive me to Sydney. I've got a gun and I'll use it.' Porter's manner had become threatening.

Although terrified, Mrs Rowley could still speak.

'I don't know who you are and I don't care. Just leave me alone. I've got to pick up my children,' she blurted out.

Porter sensed the woman would be trouble and he left the car as quickly as he had entered. Without looking where he went, Mrs Rowley drove away as fast as possible, her foot trembling on the accelerator.

John Porter knew the Gold Coast well. He was no stranger to this part of the world. In the brief times when he was neither in a welfare home or a prison, he had spent much of his time there. The woman would surely report his attack and the place would soon be swarming with police. He drove the stolen Holden to nearby Surfers Paradise. He had to get out of sight, a difficult task in the strip which was a 24-hour hive of activity. Driving slowly along Thornton Street, he entered the driveway of a block of units with the name Orly Apartments printed clearly at the entrance. He parked the car in a lower level car park and settled down, waiting for nightfall.

Porter was unintelligent and never thought or planned ahead. Acting on the spur of the moment had been the cause of all of the troubles in his lifetime. Inevitably, he would again change his mind.

Iona Abrahamson was a real estate agent, middle-aged, living with her family in the hinterland district of Coomera. She had arranged a 3.30pm appointment with a customer, Chris Smith, to discuss a property application. She drove into the Orly Apartments in her silver Datsun coupe and parked in car bay number five.

Abrahamson walked to the first floor of the apartments and was joined by Smith who was just returning from the beach. The two entered Smith's apartment and began to examine the housing applications when there was a knock on the front door.

Smith strolled casually to the door and opened it to be confronted by John Porter in his black outfit. He was holding the Browning pistol and pointing it at Smith's chest.

Porter forced his way into the unit, closed and locked the door behind him and with enormous confidence said, 'Do you know who I am? I'm John Albert Porter. Haven't you seen me on TV? Don't be alarmed. I won't be here long. I just want to get away from the police. As soon as it's dark, I'll let you go.' Porter appeared to be losing control of his emotions. On the run for ten days, the lack of food and sleep were beginning to have their effects.

Iona Abrahamson was concerned for her safety and began to prepare herself for death. John Porter was obviously unstable and his conversation spun from topic to topic.

'I'm all dressed in black because I'm the bad guy,' said Porter proudly. 'I've been in jail for eight years. I didn't want to go back. I'm going to keep running. I will have to go back for twenty years at least.'

He pointed the gun at the terrified hostages and said, 'This is what got me into trouble. My friends told me to get rid of it, but I won't.' He removed the magazine from the weapon and aimed it from Smith to Abrahamson alternatively, continually pulling the trigger. The clicking of the hammer made the victims wonder whether they were involved in a macabre game of Russian roulette.

'I should never have had this gun with me in Sydney last Monday,' Porter said. 'You know I've been on the run for a week and the media coverage has died down a bit. If I've lasted this long, it should make it easier. I nearly got away from the police in Sydney. They wanted to search me, so I punched him and shot two of them.'

Then came another tirade. 'They'll shoot me if they catch me, or they'll hang me in jail. When you're in jail, you think about how you're going to get the cops. They shot my best mate in Sydney because they thought it was me. I'm going back there to take a few more of them down.'

At 6pm, Porter turned on the radio to listen to the local news. Headlines described the attempted abduction of the woman at Southport and Porter knew that his time was limited. He grabbed the gun and shouted angrily, 'It's like a fucking pea shooter. I should have a machine gun.'

Abrahamson was carrying a personal pager and it activated. Porter became alarmed, but when he read the recorded message, he relaxed somewhat. It read, 'Iona. Ring home.'

She was allowed to ring her home, with Porter holding the gun at her head. Iona told her husband that she had almost finished her business and should be home within the hour. Having made that commitment, Porter decided that it would be better if she left, but not before threatening that he still held Smith as a hostage and his life would be endangered if she informed the police.

John Porter faced Chris Smith and said, 'If the police come, you've fucking well had it.'

Iona Abrahamson walked to the door on legs that she felt would fail her. She nervously opened the door and stepped outside, fearful that Porter would change his mind and shoot her. Once in the clear, her single thought was to get into her car and drive away from the Orly Apartments as quickly as possible.

Then a terrible reality hit her. She had left her car keys in Smith's unit. She walked to a public telephone booth outside the Northcliffe Surf Life Saving Club and telephoned her husband, this time telling him what really happened.

Detective Senior Constable Jeffrey Kelly was attached to the Broadbeach Police Station on the Gold Coast. At 7.35pm he received an urgent telephone call from Walter Abrahamson. Kelly listened to an incredible story and quickly rounded up six detectives and three unmarked police cars. A hurried briefing was held before they drove to the Northcliffe Surf Club and spoke to a still shocked Iona Abrahamson.

John Porter was edgy and nervous inside Smith's apartment and his mind turned to where he should go next— Brisbane or Sydney? He made his decision on the toss of a coin: heads for Brisbane, tails for the south. Brisbane won.

'I want you to drive me to Brisbane and drop me off at a mate's place,' Porter snapped at Chris Smith. 'I slept in a sewer last night, but I'll be safe now. The cops think I've left there.'

'I don't have much petrol. We'll have to stop at a service station,' replied Smith. 'When do you want to leave?'

'Twenty minutes,' said Porter. The time was now 8.10pm. He informed his frightened hostage, 'I've got a hot car in the car park. I don't want to use that. You're going to be my security.'

At exactly 8.30pm, the two men left the Orly Apartments, Porter behind Smith, with his gun pressed against his victim's back. They walked slowly to the basement car park. All was clear. They passed the now abandoned Holden sedan Porter had used and got into Smith's white Ford sedan, then drove slowly into Thornton Street.

Smith turned north and drove towards the main highway that would take them to Brisbane. By now, he was convinced that he would be killed, probably in a shoot-out with police. He looked in the rear-vision mirror and noticed a car was following them. He hoped it was the police. Iona would have contacted them and they would have had time to get into position.

Jeff Kelly had with him detectives John Martin, Nick StGeorge, Nick Rosata, Jim Harrison and Keith Woodbridge. Their plan was to allow Porter to drive to a less populated area of Surfers Paradise. When the car reached the Gold Coast Highway, the action began.

With their sirens blaring and blue lights flashing, the three police cars jammed Smith's vehicle—one at the front, one at the rear and one at the side. The detectives jumped from the cars, their service revolvers drawn and surrounded Porter and his terrified hostage.

Porter leapt from Smith's car and crouched in a combat position, pointing his pistol at Detective Woodbridge. The officer shouted, 'Down, down! Put the gun down or you're gone.'

Porter dropped the firearm, but then lowered himself to the ground with his hands under his body. Darkness made it hard to see what his strategy was. In fact, Porter was lying on the pistol, and as the detectives approached him, he fumbled under his body attempting to re-arm himself.

Jeff Kelly saw what Porter was up to. With three huge bounds, he landed on Porter's back and placed his gun against his head. He then retrieved Porter's firearm and shouted to his colleague, 'I've got it.'

The manhunt for John Albert Porter was over.

During the arrest Chris Smith remained in his car, waiting to be shot—either by Porter or the police. He dared not move a muscle.

Porter was handcuffed and searched. The detectives found a grey woollen sock full of bullets, a pair of scissors, a sharpened screwdriver and a torch secreted on his body. They drove the prisoner to Broadbeach Police Station.

Porter spoke only once during the journey, mumbling, 'That gun's got me into a lot of trouble. Probably I should have fought those Sydney coppers a bit more physically, then none of this would have happened. Maybe they wouldn't have looked this hungry and I might have been able to get away or something.'

The news of Porter's arrest quickly found its way to Brisbane, where two Sydney Homicide Squad detectives had been assisting in the search for the offender. They hurried to the Gold Coast to interview Porter.

His mood had changed. All he wanted to do was talk about the police shootings in Sydney. The fight had gone out of him and he was open with the detectives when they spoke with him.

Porter was charged in relation to the offences committed by him in Queensland and held in custody. A provisional warrant would be issued in New South Wales in respect of the shooting of the two Sydney officers.

THE EXTRADITION

In the morning of 5 May 1989, Constable Allan Wayne McQueen died in St Vincent's Hospital, Sydney. He had fought for life for 11 days. The charge against John Porter would now be one of murder.

At 11am, Steve Tedder once again visited his mate, but this time to fulfil the obligation of identifying the body of Allan McQueen to the police officer who would provide escort to the city morgue. Tedder made a silent promise to the still but peaceful form of his buddy: 'They've got the bastard, mate. He'll pay for this.'

A full police funeral was provided for the dead constable on 8 May 1989. Police and friends travelled to a tiny weatherboard church in Ballina for the service. Big Al was later interred in a family wall at the Ballina Cemetery, where he overlooked the rolling waves of the Pacific Ocean.

On 10 May 1989, a hearse carried the body of David Gundy to Botany Cemetery in southeast Sydney. Sixty mourners, led by Dolly Eatts, attended a private service as the body was laid to rest.

The provisional warrant for the arrest in Queensland was executed on John Porter and on 11 May 1989, proceedings for his extradition to New South Wales were commenced in the Brisbane Magistrates Court. The courtroom was packed with police, media and members of the public.

Before the matter proceeded, Porter stood in the dock and beckoned to a Sydney detective. 'I want to speak to you. When I was arrested, I was wearing a black cowboy hat. If I can have that, I won't be fighting the extradition. My solicitors want to fight it, but I don't want to be part of their fucking circus anyway. It's probably still at Broadbeach.'

The case was adjourned for an hour while the hat was retrieved, under police escort, and given to Porter.

'Thanks for that,' he said. 'I was thinking to myself, am I a man or a mouse? I'm not a mouse, so I'm going back to Sydney to face up to what I have done.'

Extradition of Porter to Sydney was granted by the Queensland Court. He was flown back by the NSW Police Air Wing and charged at Central Court with the murder of Allan McQueen and the attempted murder of Jason Donnolley and Ross Judd.

On 3 August 1990, after being convicted by a jury of each charge in the Central Criminal Court, he stood before His Honour Judge Badgery-Smith for sentence. There could only be one: penal servitude for life.

THE DAVID GUNDY ISSUE

A coronial inquest was held in Sydney inquiring into the police shooting of David Gundy. The matter was heard before the Chief Coroner, Kevin Waller, and a panel of six jurors. Eighty-nine witnesses gave evidence and 140 exhibits were tendered before the matter was completed.

The police officers were painted in a bad light by lawyers representing the relatives of Gundy and the Aboriginal community. Claims were made that the death occurred through a dangerous and illegal police raid on the house at 193 Sydenham Road, Marrickville. A motion was put to the coroner that Jim Brazel, Terry Dawson and myself should be charged with manslaughter.

The coroner considered the application, but ruled in favour of the police. On 23 August 1989, the jury retired to consider their verdict. Only a short time passed before they returned. The usual speculation took place about a jury's appearance and behaviour: eyes lowered and a failure to look at 'guilty' parties was thought by some to mean that the jury had decided against that party.

The jury took their seats, looking firmly ahead, eyes level. The foreman stood and read the verdict:

> *On 27 April 1989 at 193 Sydenham Road, Marrickville, David John Gundy died of the effects of shotgun wounds to the chest, sustained then and there near the doorway to his bedroom, when he took hold of a shotgun held by Terry Dawson, a Detective Sergeant of Police acting in the course of his duty and the weapon accidentally discharged.*

That was it. No riders or recommendations were added. The result was conclusive, the police actions had been justified. Or had they?

When the verdict was read, my eyes met those of Dolly Eatts and her legal counsel. I knew then that the inquiry into the death of David John Gundy was far from completed.

In fact, the matter was not resolved for another two years. Over that time Gundy's death had been examined by a police shooting team, the NSW Police Internal Affairs Branch, the State Ombudsman, a coronial inquiry, the Federal Court, the Full Bench of the Federal Court, the High Court of Australia, the Royal Commission Inquiring Into Aboriginal Deaths in Custody, the Director of Public Prosecutions and the Crown Solicitor. Ten authorities had become involved in some way with the incident, which was still being referred to regularly in the media as the 'bungled Gundy Raid'.

The end result came in April 1991. Each inquiry found the police had acted legally and properly.

I have visited the gravesites of Allan McQueen in Ballina and David Gundy in Botany and placed flowers at both, saddened by the manner in which these men died. The media hype is now far behind and many people have forgotten the traumatic events of April 1989. I have not, nor will I ever forget. And I will always remember Big Al.

CHAPTER TWO

I KNOW THAT VOICE

Enter any courtroom in New South Wales, from the Local Court to the High Court of Australia and look along the defence bar table. During the hearing of a case, the table is crammed with law books, their pages ready to be opened where they have been marked.

These pages contain legal precedents, set in earlier court hearings and are referred to by lawyers as 'case law' decisions. They may assist the defence or the prosecution in the presentation of their lawsuit.

One such judgment is simply referred to as *Regina v Smith*. This is the story which made that reference 'case law'.

THE BOOKIE MURDER

In 1977 the Queen's Birthday holiday fell on Monday 13 June. I was stationed at the Kogarah Police Station in the south of Sydney and held the rank of Detective Sergeant

2nd Class. I was in command of the detective strength in what was then called No. 12 Division.

I was born and bred at nearby Rockdale and so was an avid fan of the St George rugby league team. That day, the team played Parramatta in a round of the premiership and I sensed that a bad day would follow after the Saints were beaten on their home ground at Kogarah.

A bit after 11.30pm that night, the telephone rang at my home. 'Hello', I answered apprehensively.

'Good evening, boss,' came the voice at the other end of the line. 'This is Bugsy. How are you going?' 'Bugsy' was Detective Sergeant Ron Wilson who earned the nickname from his bulging, bug-like eyes.

'What's up?' I asked, familiar with his habit of casual introductions to more serious topics.

'I'm at the home of a bookmaker named Lloyd Tidmarsh. He's been shot,' came Bugsy's reply, dragging the conversation on.

'How is he?' I asked.

'Not too good. He's dead,' came his reply, seemingly pleased that I was now called back on duty. After all, Bugsy was on the night shift. Why not me too?

I drove to the crime scene at 42 Harslett Crescent, Beverley Park, a well-to-do suburb in the St George district. The dwelling was fully lit, both by the house lights and the flashing blue and red lights of the police and emergency vehicles parked at all angles outside.

I walked inside and met with Bugsy who now spoke in rapid fire while I looked and listened. On the floor near the lounge room lay the body of a middle-aged man with a number of bullet wounds to his torso.

The story unfolded. The deceased was Lloyd Joseph Tidmarsh, born 5 September 1925 who lived at that address with his wife Irene Hazel, 17-year-old daughter Michelle and 16-year-old son Michael.

Mr Tidmarsh was a highly respected registered bookmaker with the Australian Jockey Club and ran a stand in the paddock enclosures at the Sydney and Newcastle race meetings. That day, he had been working at the Randwick Holiday Carnival races before returning to his home at 5.30pm. He had dinner and moved to a back room, where he attended to records relating to his bookmaking.

Michelle had been out with her boyfriend and returned home at 9.45pm. Michael was already at home.

Mrs Tidmarsh and the children went to bed, leaving Lloyd alone watching the replay of the league match between St George and Parramatta on television.

Just before eleven o'clock, Michelle was awakened by the sound of two men speaking outside her bedroom window.

'Am I going too fast for you? Should I slow down?' asked one of the men.

'No, that's okay,' came the answer from the other.

The back door of the house was unlocked and three masked men, armed with hand guns, burst inside. One went to the hallway and shouted into the bedrooms to Mrs Tidmarsh and her daughter to stay down and leave the lights off.

Lloyd Tidmarsh moved into the lounge room to confront the intruders. He was ordered to lie on the floor. Michael left his bedroom and went to his father's aid, but he too was ordered at gunpoint to get to the floor alongside his dad. Both father and son were 'roughed up' and several demands were made by one offender to be told the location of the house safe.

'I don't have a safe,' lied Tidmarsh. 'Anyway, don't be so stupid. Didn't you know that bookies are having a bad trot at the moment?'

One of the intruders was doing all the demanding and seemed to be the ringleader. 'Where's the safe? I know you've got one,' he again demanded.

'I told you, I don't have any money,' replied the bookie.

Michael Tidmarsh was dragged to his feet and quizzed.

'Where is the safe?' screamed the intruder.

Michael was speechless. The intruder then hit the lad over the head with a piece of timber, stunning him and knocking him back to the floor.

Lloyd Tidmarsh jumped to his feet and shouted, 'Don't touch him. He's only a kid. He can't tell you anything.' He kicked a floor radiator towards the intruder and a struggle began. The bookmaker was pistol whipped and subdued. The gunman then cocked an automatic pistol and pointed it at Tidmarsh.

'Where's the safe?' came the threatening demand.

Tidmarsh again denied owning a safe. The intruder then fired four shots into the bookmaker. Once through the chest, once through the abdomen and twice through the side of his body. Lloyd Tidmarsh died instantly.

The victim's wallet was removed from his pocket as he lay dead on the floor and the three offenders ran from the house. They left the scene in what was described by a witness as a 1969 Holden station wagon, light in colour, and escaped.

The government pathologist attended the scene, as did members of the Ballistics and Scientific units. Three spent Winchester cartridges were located, as well as two .38

calibre bullets. A balaclava and stocking mask were also recovered, as well as a blue hessian bag which contained a piece of 2" x 2" hardwood, a torch and a pair of gloves.

Michael Tidmarsh was taken to St George Hospital, where he was treated for a laceration to his head. He was detained overnight for observation.

An interesting piece of evidence came to light from an interview with Michelle Tidmarsh relating to the voice of the ringleader. His voice was very distinctive—high-pitched, whining and grammatically bad. It was a voice, she said, that she would remember forever.

The usual crime scene examination took place. Witnesses were interviewed. Homicide Squad detectives were called in to assist. Exhibits were recovered. A post-mortem examination was carried out on the body of the deceased. Every effort was being made to solve this tragic, senseless murder.

Lloyd Joseph Tidmarsh was not only a well-respected person within the racing industry, but also in his private life. His death received enormous publicity and a reward was offered from the racing fraternity for information leading the to identity of the killers.

The morning following the shooting, a man travelling to work found the contents of Lloyd Tidmarsh's wallet scattered on the ground near Bexley North Railway Station, west of the crime. Club membership cards, bookmaker's licence and other personal papers, all in the victim's name, were handed to police and taken for fingerprint examination.

The contents of the hessian bag left at the crime scene were minutely examined. Invisible to the naked eye were welding spatter, hairs, vegetable matter and dirt. The samples were microscopically examined by experts from the

University of New South Wales and the Lidcombe Forensic Science Laboratory. Three months passed before an unusual and unexpected break came for the investigators.

THE BANK HOLD-UP

The South Hurstville branch of the Commercial Bank of Australia was situated in King Georges Road, South Hurstville, a southern suburb of the St George district. For some reason, this small branch was a nominated 'drop' for gate takings at weekend rugby league matches played in Sydney. A security company would deliver the cash pouches to the bank and commit them to a night safe to be picked up during the day by security staff in an armoured van. The money would then be taken to bank headquarters in central Sydney and deposited.

On 7 September 1977, as staff arrived at the bank to commence work, they were confronted at the rear door by three armed and masked men who forced their way inside. The robbers were in no hurry and patiently awaited the arrival of the manager and another staff member who both held keys and the combination to the lock on the strongroom door.

The staff were threatened by the robbers and the safe was opened. A total $180,000 in cash was stolen, reportedly the largest bank hold-up of the 1970s. As the robbers prepared to leave the bank, the security van arrived to transfer the money. One guard entered the premises, but was quickly overpowered and disarmed by the robbers.

The three robbers fled from the bank and jumped into a Holden panel van parked in a side street. There, they were challenged by a second security guard who had remained with the van. He fired two shots at the men who responded with a blast from a sawn-off shotgun before driving away.

The robbery, although large in proceeds, was clumsy in performance. While inside the bank, one offender removed his balaclava and would later be identified by staff. The type of firearms carried by the thieves, a Mauser pistol with silencer attached and two Smith and Wesson revolvers, were described to police and would also later be identified.

One offender was referred to by the name 'Frank', also a vital piece of evidence. Another, who spoke to hostage bank staff, stated that he needed the money as he was 'on the dole'. Descriptions of their clothing and a gun belt with pouch also added to the catalogue of evidence.

After escaping from the bank, the robbers drove to nearby Park Road, Carlton, where they had left a changeover get-away car, a Valiant sedan. They abandoned the panel van outside the home of a local detective sergeant who was watering his front garden. He would later identify one of the offenders. When the discarded car was searched, a bundle of banknotes totalling $2000 fell from the front seat.

THE INFORMANT

There is always someone eager to seek monetary reward for supplying vital information to police. And there are also those who do so for revenge.

A well-credentialled crook with plenty of history who mixed with the heaviest criminals was also a gig for a detective attached to the NSW Police Armed Hold-Up Squad.

The crook had been 'lashed', or cheated, on by a fellow criminal and he decided to get even. He knew who had committed the bank robbery at the CBA, and one of the men was the 'lasher'.

The informant met with his police contact and told him that a violent criminal named 'Jockey' Smith and his two accomplices—Neil Collings and Frank Montgomery—had done the job. This was of interest to the investigators, as one of the men had been referred to as 'Frank' during the robbery.

Smith was heavily armed and extremely dangerous. The gig told the detective that Smith was living in the Nowra area on the state's south coast under the assumed name of Cummings.

James Edward 'Jockey' Smith was indeed a violent criminal. He was wanted in Victoria for escaping from Pentridge Jail and had yet to answer for a number of gun-related offences in that state. He was also a suspect for shooting and seriously injuring a police officer in Sydney in January 1976 to avoid arrest.

Smith was born in Colac, Victoria, on 3 October 1942. As a youth, he became fond of horses and, for a short time, was apprenticed as a jockey in Victoria. Hence his nickname 'Jockey'. His first run-in with police came when he was 19 years old. He was arrested in Victoria for breaking, entering and stealing and sentenced to 18 months hard labour. That was the first of 25 convictions he gained for armed robbery and firearm offences.

Smith was classified as a 'heavy' criminal, although he could not be regarded as a successful one. It seemed that he was caught for every one of his crimes. James Edward 'Jockey' Smith had an extreme hatred of police.

I Know that Voice

Frank Montgomery was in his fifties and had also acquired a lengthy list of convictions. Mainly, however, as a professional shoplifter. He too had been caught many times for his crimes. Montgomery was a heavy drinker, suffered from cirrhosis of the liver and, as his age increased, so did the pain in his arthritic knees, making walking difficult. (One of the suspects in the Tidmarsh murder had been heard to say, 'Am I going too fast for you—should I slow down?') Montgomery was a close friend of Jockey's and was regarded by him as 'Grandpa'.

Montgomery lived at Marrickville, which later became of interest in the Tidmarsh murder case, as Bexley North Station, where the contents of the victim's wallet were found, was en route from Beverley Park to Marrickville. 'Monty' also owned a Valiant similar to the changeover vehicle after the bank robbery.

Neil Collings was the youngest of the three at 26, and he lived at Canterbury, also on the escape route from Beverley Park. Collings knew how to steal a car.

With the information that Smith aka Cummings was living in the Nowra area, detectives Nelson and Bowen from the CIB canvassed estate agents in the south coast country town. Finally, they had a result. A real estate agent in Junction Street, Nowra, had leased a property to a Mrs Cummings on 25 March 1977. The lease would not expire until 1 December 1977, still three months away. A photo of Jockey was shown to the estate agent who identified him as being the man she knew as Tom Cummings

The property was like a farm, large and bushy, but uncultivated. A couple of horses roamed a paddock. Called Coorong, the farmhouse was isolated and set on a

City of Canada Bay
Library Service

peninsular, with the Shoalhaven River as one boundary and a long, dirt road as the only access by land. An ideal place to observe approaches from any unwanted guests.

THE RAIDS

Having established the names and home addresses of the three suspects involved in the CBA robbery, a group of detectives drawn from the CIB and Kogarah were gathered. A decision was made that simultaneous, joint, forced pre-dawn raids would be made on those homes. Wednesday 14 September 1977 was the nominated day.

Collings and Montgomery were arrested without too much fuss in the surprise raids. Collings was protected by a couple of angry dogs, but they were soon quietened. Monty went without argument. He was recovering from a standard hangover and gave in willingly. Firearms and money, proceeds of the bank robbery, were recovered. The attempt to arrest Jockey Smith, however, was somewhat more complex.

Smith was totally paranoid about the whereabouts of any police who might be on his tail. How close to him were they? He had altered his hairstyle and grown a large, droopy moustache as a disguise. He would drive past the Nowra Police Station daily, checking if any police cars other than the local ones were present. The day before the proposed raids, Tuesday 13 September, Smith noticed a green Ford Fairlane parked at the station. This was not a local car. He became more apprehensive than usual.

Among his defence mechanisms at McMahons Road was a police radio scanner, tuned to the local frequency. Jockey listened for that odd, telltale message of a police operation. His two savage dogs barked at the slightest hint of a visitor and could be relied on to alert him of impending trouble. He also kept a number of loaded firearms handy, ready for a defence.

At 4am on 14 September 1977, Smith was awakened by the growling of his dogs. Then a voice on the radio scanner said, 'Don't speak over the radio. Go to a phone.'

That was enough warning for Jockey. It was obvious that a covert police operation was under way and he did not intend to remain in the farmhouse and welcome them. He armed himself with two hand guns, ammunition and a bag of money before taking to the bush.

Police converged on the house to discover that Jockey had given them the slip. Inside were Jockey's girlfriend Valerie June Hill and her daughter. Not to be outdone, Hill released the dogs from the house and they attacked the police. One of the dogs was subdued by gunfire and the other cowered away into bushland. Additional police were called to the house and the search for Jockey began in earnest.

I had been involved in the arrest of Neil Collings earlier that morning and had returned to Kogarah Police Station after the operation. About 6.30am, I received a telephone call informing me of Smith's escape from the Nowra raiding party. With three other Kogarah detectives, I drove to McMahons Road, North Nowra, and met with detectives Bowen, Nelson and Harding of the CIB.

I joined a search party of 50 police in cars and on foot, with helicopters in the air above. The dense bushland was interrupted by the occasional farm with an outlying barn. All these places were searched, but there was no sighting of Smith.

When the police had first arrived at the McMahons Road house, they found a Remington shotgun and a sawn-off carbine lying on the ground near the front door. Both weapons were fully loaded and cocked, ready for immediate discharge.

A search of the interior of the house revealed a cache of weapons which included Lugers, revolvers, pistols, shotguns and a stun gun. Handcuffs, gelignite, wigs, masks, stockings, walkie-talkie radios, detonators, a bulletproof vest, an ammunition belt and pouch were also found. All the accompaniments of a criminal's wardrobe. Some of the firearms would later be identified as identical to those used in the CBA robbery.

A pile of stolen goods was also located in the house. This was not unusual as Jockey was a compulsive thief. The gig who gave the police the lead had related an occasion when he and Smith were in a Chinese restaurant. After ordering their meal, Smith had left the restaurant and gone to a retail store next door. There he stole an electrical item, before returning to eat his meal.

Valerie Hill was questioned and admitted that the arsenal belonged to Jockey Smith. She also told police she had driven him to Sutherland on the day of the bank robbery, where he met up with Frank Montgomery and Neil Collings. She waited for them to drive in another vehicle to South Hurstville, commit the crime and return to her where she assisted in their escape. Hill knew they were armed, intended to commit the bank robbery and, on their return she saw the money they had stolen.

Valerie Hill was charged with being an accessory before and after the armed robbery, but it was not until

27 February 1979 that she was found guilty by a jury in Sydney's Supreme Court. She was sentenced to four and a half years' jail with a two-year non-parole period.

Montgomery and Collings were both charged with the armed robbery. Collings chose to defend the matter and went conjointly to trial with Valerie Hill. On 27 February 1979, while he and Hill were awaiting the verdict of the jury, he suffered a cardiac arrest in the cells at the Supreme Court in Darlinghurst and died.

Montgomery had decided to plead guilty and throw himself on the mercy of the court. His plea came before the others were brought to trial. He was sentenced to 10 years' hard labour, but the Grim Reaper would not spare him. His heavy drinking had sealed his fate and cirrhosis of the liver claimed him before he completed his jail sentence.

JOCKEY'S ARREST

Back at McMahons Road, North Nowra, the search for Smith was extending outwards, through thick bushland before reaching the more populated areas of Nowra and Bomaderry. It was considered by the searchers that their quarry would hide until nightfall before making a final break for freedom.

Jockey Smith was impetuous and made his move shortly after 4pm. He reached the Princes Highway in Bomaderry and was obviously panicked. After offering a female motorist money to drive him to Wollongong and being refused, he stole a child's bicycle and rode into Bunberra Street.

The local radio and TV news had been broadcasting Smith's escape and his description all day. Not only did the police know what he looked like, but now the general public also had a pretty good idea. His presence in Bomaderry was soon noticed and reported to the police.

Smith dumped the pushbike and entered a public phone box outside the Bomaderry Post Office to get himself out of sight. All this achieved was to isolate and contain him for when police arrived on the scene.

Detective Bob Godden from the CIB Armed Hold-Up Squad approached the phone box and opened the door.

'We are from the police. What is your name?' he asked Smith.

'Mike Daniels. What do you want to know for?' came the feeble reply.

'You're Jockey Smith!' Godden exclaimed.

Smith produced a .38 calibre Smith and Wesson revolver and pushed it into Godden's stomach. He pulled the trigger.

Quick thinking, lightning reactions or just plain good luck saved Godden's life. He grabbed at the gun and as he did so the webbing between his thumb and first finger slipped between the hammer and the firing pin. The weapon failed to fire. A violent struggle followed before Jockey was subdued by Godden and other officers and was handcuffed.

'You're nothing but dogs. I'll shoot the lot of you,' Jockey screamed at them.

When he was searched, police found another fully loaded pistol and a large amount of money in a bag on him. He was taken to the Nowra Police Station, where he offered the interviewing police the contents of the money bag, $2000, to let him escape.

Smith was charged with the attempted murder of Detective Godden and the armed robbery of the CBA bank in South Hurstville. He would remain in custody.

THE LINK

It was at that time that clues from the bank robbery and the murder of Lloyd Tidmarsh began to merge. Eight days after Smith's arrest, a garage proprietor in Nowra contacted police with information about a Holden station wagon that had been left with him for service by Smith, whose identity was now widely exposed through press and TV coverage. Police took possession of the vehicle, which not only resembled the 'getaway' car in the bookie's murder but numbers in the registration plate matched some of those noted by a witness.

The vehicle contained a horse bridle and blanket, both of which had hairs and oxyacetylene smattering adhering to them. An examination of the car's engine number revealed that it had been stolen.

Smith owned two horses, Dornier and Regency Head, which he kept at the North Nowra property. Examinations by independent specialists in Sydney proved that hair samples taken from the two animals matched the exhibits found in the vehicle. They were also identical with those found in the hessian bag left by the offenders at the scene of the bookmaker's murder. Threads from the hessian bag were also found in the back of the stolen vehicle.

A shed that Jockey Smith had rented in Bomaderry during his time at Nowra was searched. Offcuts of timber left at the building were handed to police by the owner and proved to be identical to the piece of timber used to batter Michael Tidmarsh on the night of his father's murder.

THAT VOICE

James Edward 'Jockey' Smith was no stranger to a court-room. Apart from the robbery of the CBA bank, he faced charges of failing to appear on a number of armed robbery offences and the attempted murder of police officer Constable Jerry Ambrose. He was also wanted in Victoria for escaping from lawful custody.

I was at Central Court on one of his appearances and, after the morning tea adjournment, a highly agitated Smith was brought into court. He protested to the magistrate that for morning tea, the police sergeant in charge of the cells had referred to him as a dog and thrown him a bone to eat.

Jockey's voice was highly pitched, almost to a scream. I discussed this with Detective Sergeant Don Worsley from the Homicide Squad who was investigating the Tidmarsh murder. Could his be the voice described by Michelle Tidmarsh as the leader of the intruders at her home on the night her father was shot?

On 23 March 1978, Michelle Tidmarsh was taken by police to the Central Court complex in Liverpool Street, Sydney. Evidence was being taken in No. 3 Court against Jockey Smith, charged with the armed hold-up of the Patrick Stevedoring Company.

Smith was conducting his own defence. He was becoming excited during the hearing and his voice was climbing.

Michelle entered the courtroom at midday and remained there for fifteen minutes. She then left and spoke to Homicide Squad detectives.

'That man's voice was the voice of the man who I heard arguing with my father about the whereabouts of the safe and where the money was in our house. His voice is definitely that of one of the men I saw,' she told them.

Four days later, Smith was charged with the murder of Lloyd Tidmarsh. The exhibits recovered from Nowra, those left at the murder scene, together with the inaugural voice identification, seemed more than sufficient to convict the suspect.

THE STALLING PROCESS

During the late 1970s, a practice had arisen in the United Kingdom of accused persons not only making verbal allegations of corruption against arresting police, but taking court process against them as well. The idea appealed to Smith. He spoke to the visiting Chamber Magistrate at Long Bay Jail, alleging a conspiracy by nine police officers involved in the murder prosecution. They were, he said, concocting a brief of untrue evidence on which to convict him.

No sworn evidence or proof needed to be given for the issue of a summons, and they were quite easily taken out against the nine officers. I know, because I received one of them. We appeared in the Central Court of Petty Sessions and the matters of alleged conspiracy were remanded.

This meant that when Smith appeared for evidence to be taken on the Tidmarsh murder inquiry, the matter would be stood over because the police involved were themselves the subject of a conspiracy allegation. Then, when the police appeared at court on that allegation, no evidence could be given as that would relate to the Tidmarsh murder and would interfere with that case. A stalemate had been reached.

Finally, after a year had passed, Smith was asked by the Magistrate what evidence he had to present against the police. He had none. The allegations were withdrawn and the police were now free to proceed with the murder charge against him.

In July 1983, in Sydney's Central Criminal Court, James Edward 'Jockey' Smith was found guilty of murdering Lloyd Tidmarsh and was sentenced to life in jail. He had already been found guilty of attempting to shoot Detective Bob Godden and was serving 14 years for that crime. He was also serving a life sentence for the attempted murder of Constable Jerry Ambrose and seven years each for three other serious, gun-related crimes. In total, Smith had booked up two life sentences and 35 years in jail. There seemed little purpose in pursuing the charge against him over the armed robbery of the CBA bank at South Hurstville and the matter did not proceed.

Jockey Smith was now out of action.

THE APPEALS

Smith appealed the Tidmarsh murder conviction to the Court of Criminal Appeal and his plea was upheld. The court found that the trial judge had erred in not properly instructing the jury in a number matters of law. A new trial was ordered.

Three years after Jockey was originally sentenced, time had taken its toll on some of the main witnesses. Detective Sergeant Don Worsley, the officer in charge of the inquiry, had died. The detective corroborating Worsley's evidence had been dismissed from the police force for misconduct and was not considered to be a reliable witness.

Application was made by Smith's lawyers for a 'no bill' of the case. The Attorney General, after considering what evidence remained, decided that a jury would not convict and he would not issue an indictment against Jockey. The murder charge was dropped.

After all his appeals against the numerous convictions had been exhausted, Jockey's time in jail would be completed after his sentence of 14 years for the shooting of Bob Godden had expired.

A CROOK TO THE END

In February 1992, Jockey Smith was released from jail on parole. He had been free for less than 24 hours when he was shot in the chest by a shotgun blast while at his flat in Bondi, in Sydney's east. Amazingly, he survived, but refused to assist police in their investigations.

Smith knew only one way in life's journey, and that was committing crime to exist. He recovered from his injuries and in November of the same year was arrested at the Erina Shopping Centre on the New South Wales central coast for shoplifting. While being escorted by store inspectors to the manager's office, he pulled a revolver from his pocket, threatened the staff and escaped.

Afraid of the criminal enemies that he had made and of the NSW Police whom he hated, Smith fled to his home state of Victoria. But nothing there changed. At 8.25pm on 5 December 1992, Jockey was again behind the wheel of a stolen vehicle, this time a Holden station wagon. He drove into the car park of the Farmers Arms Hotel in Creswick and climbed out of the vehicle. He was approached by a police officer asking for papers of ownership for the car. Smith produced a .38 calibre Smith and Wesson revolver and pointed it at the constable's head.

'I'm going to kill you!' he screamed.

A patron from the hotel had seen what was happening. He jumped into his car and drove it towards Smith. Jockey was distracted and turned away from the police officer, who drew his service pistol and fired two shots into his attacker, killing him. The high-pitched voice had been silenced.

Michelle Tidmarsh had created a precedent in Australian law with the voice identification which is now part of case law history. Two years after the murder of her father, she joined the NSW Police Force, where she remained until 2002.

CHAPTER THREE
JUSTICE TOO SWIFT

There is an old adage that passes through the legal system: 'Swift justice is good justice'. The story that follows belies that theory and proves that less haste may have brought a different and just result in a most macabre crime.

I recently attended the funeral of a friend at the huge Rookwood Cemetery in the western suburbs of Sydney. After the service, I wandered through the grounds of the necropolis looking at the years of history contained in the burial spaces. Burial grounds hold a strange fascination for me, not ghoulish, but full of interest about the life fashioned by the person no longer living. What was their life story?

The inscriptions on the gravestones and niche plaques, some ancient and some recent, each bore a similar engraving, the year of birth and the year of death. Between the two dates was a dash. What took place during that period marked with the dash?

I looked along a line of plaques on a wall of remembrance, identifying the ashes of a lost one contained in an urn within. 'Peter Tickle. 1954–1990'. I knew about that dash. Peter had been a senior constable in the NSW Police Force, attached to the Tactical Response Group. He had been severely criticised by the media in 1990 for allegedly allowing children to handle weaponry during a police exhibition at a public school. The trauma became too much for him and, despite counselling and the support of his fellow officers, Peter took his own life while in a distressed state. The dash could have told much more, about the good work and bravery of the man before his untimely death.

I rambled to the most elevated section of the cemetery, Necropolis Circuit. Memories of the past came rushing back. In 1956, almost half a century ago, I had stood in this same spot for a different reason. Looking towards East Street at the northern corner of the grounds, I could still faintly see where a rail line used to run. The line ended where I now stood, not on bare and barren ground, but at an imposing, sandstone structure, like a cathedral.

In the year 1868, those who died in the region of the City of Sydney were conveyed to Rookwood by rail. Commencing at Regent Street Mortuary Station in the city, the train carried the casket in a special, glass funeral coach, followed in separate carriages by mourners to Lidcombe, a western suburb of Sydney. There, the train would be switched to a spur line and travel into the cemetery until it reached the beautifully designed Rookwood Railway Chapel.

This style of funeral ceased in the 1940s and, in 1958, the rail line was dug up and the building sold to the Anglican Church. Stone by stone, the structure was dismantled by dedicated stonemasons, marking each block for later restructure. The heavy material was transported in 83 semitrailer loads to Ainslie, a suburb of Canberra, where it was faithfully restored to the original shape of the Rookwood Chapel. The building now stands in Cowper Street as the All Saint's Church.

The cemetery surroundings brought back memories of 1956 and where I had arrived as a constable in the NSW Police Force. In the 1950s, the Sydney metropolitan area of the NSW Police Force was divided into 20 police Divisions. No. 1 Division had its headquarters at Clarence Street, Sydney, supervising the inner Sydney area. No. 2 Division operated from Regent Street and patrolled the southwest extremity of the city. No. 3 Division looked after the notorious Darlinghurst–Kings Cross district. And so the divisions were numbered until No. 20 Division, Police Headquarters.

In August 1946, a Mobile Division was established and called No. 21 Division. Operating from rooms at the old Police Depot in Bourke Street, Redfern, the 50-man plain-clothes police had no set area of responsibility and moved from one police division to another, policing trouble spots and bringing law and order to the streets. Not only in Sydney, but in the country area of New South Wales as well. The division was known as the Flying Squad.

No. 21 Division became a training ground for prospective detectives, and it was in 1956 that I became a member of that squad. I was 25 years old and keen as mustard on becoming a detective.

'Snowy' Emerson was the boss, the Detective Inspector in Charge. His system of rostering was to work you on an afternoon shift and then bring you back the next day for the morning shift. His philosophy was that, on a late shift, if you were worth your salt, you would arrest an offender requiring you to attend court the following day.

THE CRIME

John Clarence Straughen was 30 years old and resided with his family in the western Sydney suburb of Chester Hill. He was employed in the printing trade and worked shift work. On 1 October 1956, Straughen was rostered to work a night shift in the city. He left his home at 10pm and walked the short distance to Chester Hill Railway Station, where he had five minutes to wait for his train.

In the 1950s, Chester Hill was less populated than it is today and Straughen found himself waiting alone on the railway platform. He was approached by a tall, unshaven and scruffy-looking man, aged in his thirties.

'Have you got a light, mate?' came the age-old approach from the man.

Straughen obliged, only to be faced with another request. 'Give us your wallet.'

The man was serious. He pulled a .22 calibre rifle from behind his back and poked it into Straughen's stomach. John didn't carry much money, £4 was all that he had. But it was enough for the offender. He pulled the notes from the wallet and threw it on the ground. To silence his victim, he discharged the firearm. The bullet hit Straughen in his back. The gunman then ran away, leaving his victim to die, or do the best he could for himself.

Straughen's cries for help were eventually heard by passengers on a train that pulled into the station. Police and ambulance officers were called. He was conveyed to hospital where he was admitted in a serious condition.

Straughen remained conscious during his ordeal and was able to give police a detailed account of just what had taken place. His wallet was located and taken away for fingerprint examination.

THE INVESTIGATION

At the commencement of each shift, before setting out on the day's patrol at No. 21 Division, the officers would gather in a muster room for the 'read out'. This was when descriptions of offenders wanted, registered numbers of stolen vehicles and police wireless messages would be read aloud to the assembled officers. Some messages were marked 'read' and others 'enter'. The latter would be just that, entered into the officer's notebook for easy reference. To ensure that each officer complied with this routine, the notebook would be checked and signed by a senior officer after each read out.

A description of John Straughen's attacker was marked 'enter' and was recorded in my notebook. The read out completed, the evening's duty roster would be called. I was detailed to patrol the Chester Hill area, which meant sitting alone at railway stations acting as a decoy, hoping that the offender would revisit his crime scene.

Chester Hill Railway Station was one of many on the Liverpool rail link and the nearby stations of Regents Park, Sefton, Bass Hill and Yagoona were also pinpointed for surveillance. Quite a few lonely nights were spent patrolling these stations, but to no avail.

Detectives from the CIB had taken over the investigation and they were rewarded with a breakthrough. The fingerprints lifted from John Straughen's wallet had been identified. The suspect was 35-year-old John Henry Fishburn aka John Fisher. Fishburn was a drifter, a vagrant with a number of convictions for street offences, but nothing as serious as the situation he now faced. A complete description of Fishburn, including identifying tattoos, was marked in the wireless messages as 'enter'.

Two weeks had passed since the shooting and there was no sighting of the suspect. On 15 October 1956, I was rostered to work an afternoon shift, 3pm until 11.30pm, at No. 21 Division with another detective hopeful, Alan Pry. Our patrol that evening was the No. 3 Division (Darlinghurst) and the adjoining No. 10 Division (Paddington).

We patrolled in an unmarked police car, locked up a few offenders for indecent language and offensive behaviour and decided to get a few names of crooks who were consorting with each other. The Consorting Act had been introduced, making it unlawful to knowingly associate with a fellow criminal. If six or more 'bookings' over a period of three months were recorded against a criminal, he could be arrested and charged with consorting. The offence carried a six-month jail sentence as a penalty.

The wine bars and hotels around the Haymarket area of the city were frequented by the 'crims' and always provided a few bookings. From there, we moved on to 64 Foster Street, Surry Hills, the Salvation Army refuge for homeless and unemployed men. Accommodation was limited at the refuge and a bed and a plain meal would be provided to those lucky enough to secure a place in the queue. A ticket would be issued to the men who would wait eagerly for the door to open at 6pm.

Alan Pry and I walked into Foster Street at 5.45pm. The street was short and narrow and the dishevelled men were gathered closely together, not wanting to be edged out of the line. We began taking names. I approached one man. He was about six feet tall, unshaven and reeked of body odour.

I asked the man the standard opening question: 'We're from the police. What's your name?'

'John Fisher,' he replied.

'Have you been in trouble with the police before?' This was the second routine question.

'A bit,' he said.

The name John Fisher suddenly rang a bell. I turned back the pages in my notebook until I came to the description of John Henry Fishburn, alias John Fisher. The wireless message listed a number of identifying tattoos on the suspect, one being of a large, red Indian's head complete with feather headdress on his right forearm.

'Let's have a look at your right forearm,' I ordered. The arm was bared and I looked down at the Indian head tattoo. I was talking to John Henry Fishburn.

We quickly arrested and searched Fishburn, but no firearm was found. We drove our prisoner to the Criminal Investigation Branch, which was then situated above the Central Police Station in Central Lane. As the novices, we called out the officer in charge of the investigation, Detective Sergeant Jack Bateman.

THE 'RUN AROUND'

Bateman was a likeable man and a leading Homicide investigator of that time. He was happy to allow me to tag along as an observer for what was to follow. Perhaps I might learn something. This courtesy was so unlike many other senior detectives who would dismiss junior officers and take complete control of the arrested man. Jack Bateman was not one of these.

Fishburn was easy to interview. He held nothing back and freely admitted to the shooting of John Straughen. He was broke and needed money. Shooting the man did not worry him, it was a necessity.

As is still the case, the handcuffed offender was taken on a 'run around'. Back to the scene of the crime for a re-enactment of what he had done and what followed after the shooting.

We stood on Chester Hill Railway Station, coincidentally at 10pm, the same time as when the offence had been committed a fortnight earlier. Fishburn described how he approached his victim, stole his wallet and shot him. What followed then was nothing short of bizarre.

'What did you do then?' asked Jack Bateman.

'I went home,' Fishburn replied.

'And where was that?' asked the detective.

'I'll show you. It's a long walk.'

Fishburn headed to the end of the railway platform and jumped onto the railway track. We followed him along the permanent way for five kilometres until we reached Lidcombe Railway Station. A spur line ran from the main track into Rookwood Cemetery. We followed that line well into the graveyard until we reached an imposing, cathedral-like sandstone structure—the Rookwood Railway Chapel.

Fishburn walked about 50 metres off the rail line to a row of mausoleum buildings, family crypts. He picked up an iron bar from where it lay hidden in long grass and gently eased open the steel door to one of the vaults. Squeaking on the verdigris that had accumulated over the years made the whole procedure seem like we were participating in a horror movie.

'This is my home,' Fishburn said casually, seemingly oblivious of the gruesome setting.

We shone our torches into the tomb and followed him into its ghastly interior. The air was rank and stale. I made sure the door remained open, not primarily for the sake of fresh air.

On each side of the chamber lay a coffin covered in dirty blankets. These were Fishburn's beds. On one coffin was a .22 calibre rifle.

Fishburn indicated the rifle and said, 'That's what you're looking for.'

Back at Central Police Station, John Fishburn was further interviewed and made a full, written confession to the shooting. The firearm he used had been stolen from a house he'd broken into in the Lidcombe area. The money stolen from Straughen was spent on food and, because Fishburn was now penniless he had gone to the Salvation Army refuge for a free meal and a bed for the night.

John Henry Fishburn was charged with shoot with intent to murder John Clarence Straughen. Bail was refused and he was remanded in custody.

The shooting left John Straughen paralysed for life from the waist down. He was pleased that his attacker had been caught, but his health was poor and his paralysis caused him major distress. John's sworn evidence was taken at his bedside and admitted into evidence at the lower court committal proceedings.

THE STING

On 28 November 1956, after taking evidence at the Central Court of Petty Sessions, Fishburn was committed to stand trial on the charge of attempted murder that had been preferred by the police. Instead, the Attorney General, on the advice from the Director of Public Prosecutions, arraigned Fishburn on two charges of robbery being armed and malicious wounding.

On 1 April 1957, five months after the shooting, Fishburn appeared in the Central Criminal Court. He pleaded guilty to the two charges and was sentenced to 10 years' hard labour on the robbery charge and five years for the wounding of Straughen. Both sentences were to be served concurrently.

John Straughen felt that the sentence was incompatible with the crime and said, 'He got five years for shooting me. I got life in a wheelchair.'

The result was also disappointing for the police who thought that the original charge of attempted murder should have been pursued. That sense of disappointment deepened when, in July 1957, just nine months after he had been shot, John Straughen passed away. The cause of death was found to have resulted from the gunshot wound inflicted by Fishburn.

SOMETHING LEARNED

The legal proofs of murder are straightforward. The act causing the death of the victim has to be committed by the offender. John Fishburn had been proven to be that person. The act had to be malicious. That also had been proved. The death of the victim had to occur within a year and a day of that act. Straughen had died within that time period. All the proofs for a murder conviction were there, but the matter had been finalised.

If more consideration had been given to the health of Straughen and his prognosis for life, a less hasty approach could have been taken in the legal proceedings against Fishburn. Charged with murder, and convicted, he would have faced a life sentence.

John Henry Fishburn lived for another 29 years. His 'home' in a cemetery while he was alive had become his permanent place of residence.

CHAPTER FOUR
FOOL'S GOLD

Murray Frederick Farquhar was described in an article published in the *Sydney Morning Herald* as 'a bright boy from Broken Hill who rose to become NSW Chief Magistrate and, later the first Australian judicial officer to go to prison'. He was born in Broken Hill on 7 July 1918. In 1936 he entered the NSW Public Service as a clerk. During World War II he served with the AIF in the 2/48th Infantry Battalion and saw action in the Middle East and Indonesia. He rose to the rank of captain before he was demobilised at the end of the war.

Farquhar then studied law and was appointed as a magistrate in 1962. In 1971 he became Chief Magistrate. He was flamboyant and received unwanted publicity on several occasions. In 1978 he was photographed sitting in the Members' Stand at the Randwick Racecourse alongside well-known criminal George Freeman and Nick Paltos, who was later to be convicted of drug trafficking.

In 1985 Murray Farquhar was found guilty in Sydney's Supreme Court of attempting to pervert the course of justice. This related to his attempt to influence a fellow magistrate in a criminal matter. He was sentenced to four years' hard labour and was released after 10 months.

In 1991, Farquhar again hit the headlines when he was charged with the possession of valuable paintings stolen from the Melbourne home of millionaire Samuel Smorgon. He was acquitted of the charge. The next time his name appeared in the papers was for an amazing story.

'Fool's Gold Sting which Fooled Farquhar—an Incredible, Crazy, Insane, Madcap Scheme' was the head-line of an article published in the *Sun-Herald* newspaper on 30 January 1994. Written tongue-in-cheek, the story summarised a scheme to steal $8 billion in gold bars from the Philippines. The scheme involved Murray Farquhar, three representative rugby league football stars, a decommissioned Royal Australian Navy minesweeper manned by armed mercenaries and two former disgraced members of the NSW Police Force.

THE PLAN

Post Enterprised and Supplies was a factoring and broker-age company operating from the Sydney offices at 90 Foveaux Street, Surry Hills. The two principal directors were Peter Rockingham Cartwright and Anthony James Wardle, both of whom had had their share of trouble with the law.

Peter Cartwright had been a member of the NSW Police Force, but was dismissed after being charged with being knowingly concerned in the importation of heroin and possession of heroin. On his conviction in 1985, he was sentenced to 14 years' hard labour with a non-parole period of eight years.

Wardle was a qualified accountant and met his business partner in jail while he was serving a period of detention for dishonesty. On his release from prison, he assumed the name of Tony Evans. Both men were released from jail for good behaviour well before their sentences expired.

They agreed to form a partnership in the factoring business, which operated legitimately and under the supervision of the Federal Probation and Parole Service. Cartwright and Evans were both now in their late thirties, and still had time to re-establish their careers and live in a law-abiding manner.

In stark contrast, a brokerage company trading as Crystal Promotions of Croydon had as the senior director a criminal named Gerald Kron. The company was a front for any illegal transaction that could be entered into. Kron resided at the southern suburb of Sydenham and could simply be described as a con man. He had gathered a number of convictions for false pretences, conspiracy and forgery, among other charges.

His partner in business was, coincidentally, another former NSW Police officer, Thomas Morrison, who still carried his police identification certificate which he had failed to surrender on his discharge. Morrison knew Peter Cartwright when both were serving police officers and he was aware of Peter's trouble over the 1985 drug importation. Morrison set out to involve Cartwright and his partner Evans in a scheme that had all the trappings of a James Bond adventure.

Early in February 1990, Thomas Morrison and Gerald Kron—later to use the codenames 'Tom' and 'Jerry'—regularly visited Cartwright at his place of business with offers to dispose of stolen property through his company. They anticipated that Cartwright would agree to the proposals because of his earlier criminal experience. The opposite, however, occurred. Cartwright was petrified of being detected and being returned to jail. He was on parole and had no wish to forfeit that privilege.

Morrison and Kron persisted, claiming they had access to unlimited numbers of computers, facsimile machines, electronic equipment, photocopiers and a shipping container of high-quality, tinned red salmon. All the property was stolen and, if moved through Post Enterprised and Supplies, good profit could be gained by all those involved. Whether these approaches were to test Cartwright in any thoughts he might have about reporting the matter to law authorities was left to conjecture. He decided to listen to what might eventuate and then quietly report the matter to his parole officer.

Cartwright and Evans managed to stall Tom and Jerry until 23 February 1990. They didn't want to get involved any further. Evans knew an officer in the Australian Federal Police and the story was relayed to him. As the matter was of a State concern, the inquiry came to detectives at my office at the Sydney Police Centre in Goulburn Street.

The officers listened with interest to Cartwright as he related the information. No material evidence yet existed to warrant any criminal charges. Cartwright and Evans agreed to report any further developments. Both were registered as NSW Police informants in accordance with the existing policy. A case officer was appointed, who would liaise with the two men.

Morrison and Kron took a lease on an office in the same Surry Hills premises to be closer to Cartwright and Evans. Shortly after taking occupancy, a file containing copies of gold certificates was stolen from the office of Post Enterprised. The certificates concerned the sale of a large amount of gold. Evans had been holding the certificates since 1983, and would use them to verify his knowledge of gold transactions. They could be used to show that Evans was professionally equipped with the knowledge required for the identification and purity of gold, as well as to purchase and sell the valuable metal.

In April 1990, Morrison and Kron approached Cartwright with a different scheme. They invited Cartwright and Evans to meet a man named Murray Farquhar who had devised a plan to steal a large quantity of gold from the Philippines and move it to Dubai in the United Arab Emirates. Kron spoke of a military coup in the Philippines and the gold would be stolen during this uprising. Kron said he was aware that Evans and Cartwright had a full understanding of the documentation involved with gold transactions and their participation in the scheme was because of this knowledge.

Murray Frederick Farquhar was then 72 years old and resided at Beach Street, Coogee, in the eastern suburbs. He had retired from the position of NSW Chief Magistrate in 1979 and had been under remand on a charge of possessing stolen, valuable artwork.

Cartwright came to my office at the Sydney Police Centre and told me of the new developments. A Supreme Court warrant was obtained for use of a listening device. The gadget was placed in a briefcase, which would be carried to the meeting with Farquhar.

At 1.30pm on 19 April 1990, at the up-market dining establishment of Dimitri's Five Doors Restaurant in Surry Hills, a meeting took place between Peter Cartwright, Tony Evans, Gerald Kron and Murray Farquhar. Evans had with him the briefcase containing the listening device. Two undercover officers from the NSW Police sat at an adjacent table, making observations of their targeted group.

The meeting was a sounding out, introductory affair with free-and-easy conversation among the four men. Farquhar set the theme of the discussion. A large amount of gold bullion was held in the Philippines and he and Kron had commenced negotiations to obtain it illegally. An armed vessel would soon be in Philippine waters to assist in the removal of the gold. As the conversation proceeded, Cartwright and Evans began to suspect that Kron and Farquhar were in possession of the stolen certificates from their office.

The talk shifted to well-known criminals Lennie McPherson and George Freeman, who Farquhar described as 'good blokes' and his friends. No doubt this was said to impress those present. The meeting concluded with arrangements made to get together the following Saturday at the Coogee Randwick RSL Club, where more detailed plans would be made.

Cartwright and Evans proceeded to a meeting with their police case officer. They reported the contents of their discussions at Dimitri's and returned the listening device.

It was common knowledge that a large amount of gold, previously in the possession of the deposed President

Ferdinand Marcos, had been secreted in the jungles of the Philippines and remained there after Marcos was exiled from his country. This was thought to be the gold referred to by Murray Farquhar.

At 11.30am on Saturday 21 April 1990, Cartwright and Evans arrived by taxi at the Coogee Randwick RSL Club. The doorman seemed to be expecting the two men and they were ushered into a private room. Farquhar was already there and Kron arrived shortly afterwards. Then followed an extraordinary discourse that stunned both Cartwright and Evans.

A military coup to overthrow the Philippine government was imminent. Farquhar planned to utilise the unrest and confusion that would follow to launch his own attack on the Central Bank of Manila and remove 500 tonnes of gold bullion. The estimated value of the haul was $8 billion. As Farquhar had prior military experience, he declared himself the commander of the Australian raiding party.

Codenames were issued. Farquhar was 'Brush', Rocky Cartwright would be 'Stone', Tony Evans 'Bullwinkle' and Kron would be 'Crown'. The Philippines would be referred to as 'Phillips Country' and the gold as 'shrimp'. False passports would be obtained for the group and referred to as 'The Family Albums'. The cost of each passport would be $5000.

Kron then informed the meeting that influential people would be involved in the coup and would assist Farquhar's attack on the bank. Cardinal Sin and Ponce Enrile were two names mentioned, even though they were considered loyal to President Aquino.

Should any trouble be encountered on the wharves during the loading of the gold onto the waiting ships, a counterattack would be mounted. The ships would be armed with ground-to-air missiles for protection and the Philippine revolutionaries would be paid in gold bars for their assistance.

Farquhar concluded the meeting by announcing, 'When we reach open waters, our commandos will protect us from the ocean pirates. We will be given safe passage to Dubai. In the meantime, I will make arrangements to ensure finance. Remember, gentlemen, trust, honour and loyalty to each other must be maintained at all times and each codename must be used at all times on the telephone and in general conversation.'

The finance Farquhar referred to was the sum of $100,000, which he would forward to Australia after his arrival in Dubai.

The meeting concluded and the two informants travelled to the city, met with their case officer and handed him the recorded contents of the conference.

THE MOVE BEGINS

The Monday following the meeting at the RSL club, Cartwright received a telephone call in his office from Murray Farquhar.

'Stone, it's Brush. Can you and Bullwinkle and come to the international airport, Singapore Airlines section at 12.45pm today?' Farquhar was on his way.

Cartwright and Evans drove to the airport, where they spoke with Farquhar. Evans was told that he would soon be required to travel to Manila to meet an accomplice who was employed at the Central Bank of Manila. The onus would be placed on Evans to identify the hallmarks on the gold, assess the amount of bullion held at the bank and its purity. Two vessels, the *Teal* and *Sprightly*, under the control of Farquhar, were now crewed by armed commandos and would soon be in waters off the Philippines ready to link up with the rebels when the uprising commenced.

The former Chief Magistrate aka 'Brush' then handed some papers to Evans and said, 'I believe these are yours.' They were the gold certificates missing from Evans' office.

Farquhar departed Sydney at 2.15pm on Singapore Airlines flight SQ222, en route to Singapore. He would then transfer to a connecting flight to Dubai, where he was booked into the Ramada Hotel.

The ships referred to by Farquhar were identified by police. The *Teal* was a former Royal Australian Navy minesweeper, decommissioned in 1978. The vessel had since had several owners and was used as a charter boat and later for salvage operations. She certainly had the capability to sail on the high seas. Latest maritime records showed that the *Teal* was then in Papua New Guinea waters.

Sprightly was an ocean-going tug and had recently undergone a $1 million refit in Melbourne. The ship was berthed at Cairns harbour, in north Queensland, taking on stores before sailing for Philippines waters to carry out an alleged salvage operation.

Meetings and telephone conversations, both local and international, were constant between Kron, Cartwright, Evans and Farquhar. Codenames were being used with most information being legally intercepted and recorded. NSW detectives compiled a running sheet that grew in thickness daily. A crime analyst was committed to the inquiry and prepared a graph and link chart of those involved and of new recruits to the conspiracy.

A number of businessmen showed interest in purchasing the gold bullion that was being offered by Gerald Kron at bargain prices, no questions asked. Three rugby league representative footballers invested in the scheme, one of them contributing $60,000.

The purchase price offered by Kron was such that doubts would exist over the lawfulness of the transaction. But however fanciful the plot appeared, it was up and running and progressing at a rapid speed.

THE SCENARIO

The evidence obtained by the informants revealed that an alleged uprising would take place in the Philippines in order to overthrow President Aquino. The Central Bank of Manila would be attacked by rebels, assisted by a group of invading commandos under orders from Murray Farquhar. Five hundred tonnes of gold bullion would be stolen and transferred to waiting vessels in the nearby harbour. The gold would be taken to Dubai in the United Arab Emirates and sold to prospective buyers, some of whom had already become involved. Payment to the Philippine rebels who assisted in removing the bullion from the bank would be in gold bars.

One hundred thousand dollars had already been placed in a bank account to be operated by the informants Cartwright and Evans. A portion of that money would be used to obtain false Australian passports for Farquhar, Kron, Thomas Morrison, Cartwright and Evans. Other money would cover the airfare of Evans, who was to travel to the Philippines prior to the coup to establish the quality and quantity of the gold.

The motor tug *Sprightly* was being prepared in Cairns and would convey a party of Australian mercenaries to assist in the coup and the removal of the gold. The tug was purported to be used for the search, location and salvage of sunken shipping wrecks in the China Sea and permission had been obtained from the Australian government to carry firearms aboard, allegedly for protection against ocean pirates.

The time had arrived when higher authorities should be alerted. Both the NSW and Federal governments were advised of the situation. The Foreign Affairs Minister, Senator Gareth Evans, advised President Aquino in a confidential communique.

Mrs Aquino wasted no time and dispatched the head of her Presidential Security Group, Captain Emmanuel Andaya, to Sydney. I met with him and briefed him on the outlandish plan. The captain was the only person who kept a straight face when informed of the plan. He simply replied that Manila was only 12 minutes' drive from the seaport and the plan to steal gold in the manner described was, in fact, quite possible. The suggestion that Cardinal Sin and Ponce Enrile could be involved came as no surprise to Andaya. He said that anything was possible in the Philippines.

The captain was most interested in obtaining the names of the Australians who were planning the operation and the NSW Police were of the opinion that, if the men were detected in his country, heavy action would be swift.

Meanwhile Farquhar, now in Dubai, had commenced arrangements for his participation in the coup. He purchased a military uniform and a tin of bootpolish to blacken his face as a basic form of disguise. He visited the Apollo Photographic Studio where, clean-shaven and bespectacled, he obtained six passport-sized photographs and a negative of himself. He mailed the photos to Kron in Sydney, requesting he obtain a false Australian passport for him in the name of John Dier with the date of birth 25 April 1924.

Another player now entered the conspiracy: Donald Ross Lawton, aged 62, of Duke Street, Campsie, in Sydney's inner west. Lawton was a friend of Gerry Kron and had a short criminal history of fraud and firearm offences. He also had a contact who was employed within the Sydney headquarters of the Registrar For Births, Deaths and Marriages, making it possible for full birth certificates of any living or deceased persons to be obtained. These would be necessary for the subsequent obtaining of the false passports. Lawton was given the task of obtaining those documents.

Rocky Cartwright was instructed to obtain a false passport. He was on parole and not permitted to leave Australia—not that he wanted to—but he had to go along with the arrangements or risk discovery as an informant.

Donald Lawton and Gerry Kron visited cemeteries and from tombstones selected the names of people born around the same years as the conspirators, one of which could be used by Cartwright. The name Gary George Blake was selected and a birth certificate obtained. However, they discovered that Blake had previously held an Australian passport, so his name was discarded.

Gerry Kron decided to involve his daughter Joanna in the conspiracy. She had a relationship with a man named William Leslie Robertson, and supplied her father with Robertson's Medicare card and other personal papers and forms of identification. Robertson was unaware of what was going on.

Rocky Cartwright had the necessary passport-sized photographs taken and gave them to Tom Morrison. Morrison was a cunning operator and had maintained his friendship with a number of NSW Police officers with whom he had worked before he left the force, no doubt as a means of prevailing upon them if the circumstances warranted a favour.

Morrison went to a city hotel where he bought a couple of drinks for one of those police officers. He asked the senior sergeant if he would endorse a passport application for a mate. The officer agreed and unwittingly signed the backs of the photographs of Cartwright and endorsed the proof of identity declaration on the passport application in the name of William Leslie Robertson. The favour would have serious consequences on the career of the senior sergeant.

Money continued to pour in from prospective investors for their share of gold bullion. The cash flow wasn't only one way, it had also to go out. Telephone expenses for overseas and local calls became extreme. Members of the conspiracy party, not including the two informants, flew first class to Manila and Hong Kong. Through the services of Interpol and the Australian Federal Police liaison officers, surveillance of the suspects was maintained, filmed and forwarded to NSW Police investigators.

The maritime authorities in Cairns had been made aware of the activities proposed for *Sprightly* and kept my office informed of all that took place, on or about the vessel. The *Sprightly* and its crew had come under prior police notice 12 months earlier in Papua New Guinea waters. Suspicion was that the crew were involved in the exporting of firearms.

On 26 June, *Sprightly* sailed from Cairns harbour with a crew of twenty. Its destination was the Philippines. The vessel arrived in Labuan, in Malaysia, on 9 July and the name *Sprightly*, which appeared on the bow of the ship was painted over in the same colour as the hull to avoid surveillance. The tug then continued on to Singapore, arriving on 15 July.

Two crew members deserted the ship in Singapore and reported to the Australian Federal Police at the Australian Embassy. Coincidentally, two NSW detectives were in Singapore on an unrelated matter and they attended the embassy. The deserters reported that the vessel was carrying more weapons than it was authorised. They also informed the police of the ship's mission.

I dispatched two Sydney detectives to Singapore, where they liaised with local authorities. The *Sprightly* was docked off Loyang Offshore Supply Base. A decision was made that the vessel should not be allowed to proceed to the Philippines and now was the time to commence action.

On the morning of 25 July, the *Sprightly* was boarded by Singaporean Police, customs officers and port personnel accompanied by the two Sydney detectives. Army explosive experts with sniffer dogs were utilised in a search of the vessel. A cache of weapons was seized which included:

- ten 9mm automatic pistols
- six Chinese 7.62 semi-automatic rifles
- six pump-action shotguns

- seven spear guns and crossbows
- nine daggers
- 4000 rounds of ammunition
- 3000 metres of detonating cord
- 1000 metres of safety fuse, and
- 100 detonators.

Trolleys, banding machines and rolls of tar paper in which the gold bars were to be packaged and concealed were also seized. None of the property had been declared.

The captain of the *Sprightly* and three officers were arrested and provisionally charged with trafficking in firearms and explosives. When interviewed, the men told police that the *Sprightly* was to leave Singapore and sail to the port of Ceba in the Philippines, where the captain would receive final instructions concerning the transportation of a large amount of gold bullion out of the country.

Charges against the crewmen were later altered to unlawful possession of firearms and explosives. A fine of $10,000 was imposed, the firearms and explosives were confiscated and the *Sprightly* was impounded.

The second vessel, the *Teal*, on becoming aware of the fate of her sister ship, stayed well away from Philippine waters.

WHAT OFFENCES HAD BEEN COMMITTED

Legal discussions took place in Sydney between NSW Police and both Federal and State Directors of Public Prosecutions to establish what offences had been committed in the jurisdiction of New South Wales. Had a criminal conspiracy taken place? Surprisingly, the answer was 'no'. To plan a crime in New South Wales that was to take place in an overseas country, although morally wrong, could not be held to be criminally wrong. Case law precedents stated that an agreement in one country to commit an offence in another held no jurisdiction relative to a charge of Conspiracy.

The Commonwealth legislation of *Crime and Foreign Incursions and Recruitment Act 1978* was considered. To proceed under this Act, the consent of the Federal Attorney General was required. The Commonwealth Director of Public Prosecutions decided against this prosecution as facts could not be established sufficiently to prove that armed Australians had been trained in this country with a view of an incursion into a foreign country to engage in hostile activities.

There was, however, strong evidence direct from the informants Cartwright and Evans, supported by listening device material and telephone intercepts, that Murray Farquhar, Gerry Kron, Joanna Kron, Donald Lawton and Thomas Morrison were involved in a conspiracy to obtain false Australian passports, an offence under Commonwealth legislation carrying a penalty of imprisonment for a period of five years or a fine of $10,000. Accordingly, indictments were prepared.

On 9 July 1990, Murray Farquhar returned to Sydney from abroad and was arrested several days later. Gerald Kron, Donald Lawton, Thomas Morrison and Joanna Kron were each arrested at their respective homes and charged with conspiracy.

On 26 July, the senior sergeant from the NSW Police Force who wrongfully signed the passport application and photos of the person purporting to be William Leslie Robertson was interviewed by police from the Internal Affairs Branch. The officer was charged with making a false declaration under the *Passport Act 1938* (Cwlth) and dismissed from the force. He was subsequently found guilty of the charge in the Commonwealth Court and sentenced to nine months in custody. The former police officer appealed the sentence, which was later varied to serve 400 hours of community service.

On 3 December 1993, during his trial in the Sydney District Court, Murray Newton Farquhar suffered a heart attack and later died in hospital. The remaining offenders each pleaded guilty to their charges and were sentenced as follows: Joanna Kron—to enter recognisance to be of good behaviour for 12 months; Thomas Morrison—400 hours of community service; and Gerald Kron—nine months' periodic detention. Donald Lawton was ordered to enter a recognisance in the sum of $1000 to be of good behaviour for three years.

The footballers, businessmen and other willing contributors to the purchase of the gold may have had prima facie evidence established against them, but the possibility of conviction was remote. They would be called as witnesses, having already suffered a large monetary setback when their investment was squandered by the principal offenders.

What began as a game of espionage might well have eventuated had the players been allowed to continue. The adage of 'prevention is better than cure' resulted in several benefits: President Aquino remained in command of the Philippines, the *Sprightly* and its well-armed crew were taken out of the action and penalised, 500 tonnes of gold bullion remained in the Central Bank of Manila, and five offenders and a number of potential receivers had their wings clipped.

CHAPTER FIVE
SHOCK WAVE

Hatred is the invisible ingredient of terrorism that has no boundaries. In 1979, a small terrorist group calling themselves '15 May' was formed, setting up their headquarters in Baghdad, Iraq. The organisation had become disenchanted with the moderate views of Yassah Arafat, leader of the Palestine Liberation Organisation in his opposition to Israel.

The group took their name from the date in 1949 when Israel became a state. Their main objective was the advancement of the Palestinian cause. This would be achieved by coercing and intimidating, by means of force and violence, personal injuries to civilians and causing economic damage to Israeli interests worldwide. The United States of America, and any other country supporting Israel, were automatic targets of 15 May.

Abu Ibraham was the elected leader with the pseudonym of 'Bomb Man'. He planned the terrorist bombing locations and prepared devices for such missions. Mohammed Rashed and Christine Pinter were members selected as couriers to travel the world and deliver these devices to international associates or 'sleepers'.

Much is publicised today about world terrorism and how Australia could well be a target. In reality, we have been a target for decades. This story has its origin in Sydney in 1982, over 20 years ago.

Westfield Towers was an impressive building, one tower being totally occupied by the exclusive Boulevard Hotel, the other consisting of 15 levels of office suites. Situated at 100 William Street, Sydney, the structure was in the heart of the commercial section of the busy central business district.

In 1982, Westfield Towers housed a number of prominent and noted business personnel. Two former Australian Prime Ministers occupied separate suites, the Chief Executive Officer of the Westfield Development chain, another. The elite NSW–Federal Police Joint Drug Task Force operated from the eighth level under the name of Delta Industries. The Royal Commission of Inquiry Into Drug Trafficking had offices in the complex. On the seventh level were several suites occupied by the Israeli Consulate.

About 2pm on 23 December, the city was filled with people hurriedly finalising their Christmas shopping. The Boulevard Hotel was completely booked out with holiday guests. Office workers, returned from their lunchbreaks, were settling at their desks in the adjoining tower.

The blast erupted from a briefcase that had been carried like an everyday accessory into the building. The explosion was enormous. Concrete stairs in Westfield Towers were reduced to rubble, ceilings were brought down, heavy doors were blown off their hinges, waterpipes ruptured and a hole ripped through a 40cm thick concrete floor on the seventh level.

Robert Cester was at his desk on the sixth level office of an insurance group. He was thrown across the office by the force of the explosion, his shirt blown off his back, and lay covered in dust and debris falling from the ceiling. It was a miracle that he escaped serious injury.

Kara Lowy, a 70-year-old tea lady, was working in the Israeli Consulate on the seventh level, the seat of the explosion. She wasn't so lucky. Her injuries included a fractured skull, four broken ribs, a broken leg and bruising. Although seriously injured, Kara would survive.

Dr Moshe Liba, the Israeli Consul General, was absent from the building, as were most of his staff, minimising human injury. Structural damage to the building, however, was immense.

Emergency services rushed to the scene, evacuating the occupants and transferring the injured to hospital. The question on everyone's lips: 'Was the explosion caused by electrical or gas faults?' The answer was neither.

Investigations by crime scene experts from the NSW Police revealed smatterings of a plastic explosive against the fire wall of the Israeli Consulate. This was later identified as pentareathirite terinitrate (PETN). Contained in a briefcase and activated by a timing device, this explosion was no accident but a deliberate attack on the consulate.

A SECOND ATTACK

At 5pm the same day, a 1971 Valiant sedan was driven into the car park of the Hakoah Social Club in O'Brien Street, Bondi, in Sydney's eastern suburbs. The parking area was situated below the members' lounge and the driver had little difficulty in locating a car space. The old car seemed in stark contrast to other more luxury cars nearby.

The driver opened the boot of the car which contained two 30 pound, fully charged liquid petroleum gas cylinders, lying head-to-toe against each other. A small container of petrol sat against the cylinders with four explosive detonators, crimped to a fuse, dangling inside. The other end of the fuse wire was attached to a timing device that would be remotely activated by a power pack of two triple-A batteries. The driver opened the valves on the necks of the gas cylinders, setting off a hissing sound as the gas began to escape, each venting their contents onto the other.

The timing device was set to activate in one hour, sending a charge to the detonators and sparking a petrol fire. This would ignite the escaping propane gas, directing the flames onto each cylinder to create a BLEVE or a boiling liquid expanding volume explosion, an extremely powerful blast.

The driver closed the door of the Valiant and proceeded up the stairway into the licensed club area. Inside were many members and guests enjoying the Christmas festivities.

The clock on the member's bar wall stopped at 6.30pm as the explosion erupted from the Valiant's boot in the car park below. Sweeping sideways through the car park, cars crumpled before the fiery progression. A large, rough-edged hole appeared in the 35cm, reinforced concrete floor of the club as the BLEVE fought to find freedom from the confined area of the car park. The ignited gases sped through the club lounge to the front foyer, tossing the heavy entrance doors from their tracks as the shock waves escaped into the street. Several club patrons were injured, none fatally. Damage to the Hakoah Club and members' motor vehicles was massive.

News of the second explosion reached the NSW Police officers still investigating the crime scene at the Westfield

TACTICAL INTELLIGENCE SECTION

ARMED HOLDUP UNIT

PERSONAL PROFILE

on.

JOHN ALBERT EDWARD **PORTER**

FULL NAME :- **PORTER @ STEVENS** JOHN ALBERT EDWARD

DATE OF BIRTH :- **26.06.61**

NSW Police profile on John Porter.

Above: Murray Farquhar's photos for a false passport
in the name of John Dier.

Opposite: Edward 'Jockey' Smith's body lying beside the
police vehicle where he was fatally shot.

Wreckage of the car bomb in the car park of
Sydney's Hakoah Club.

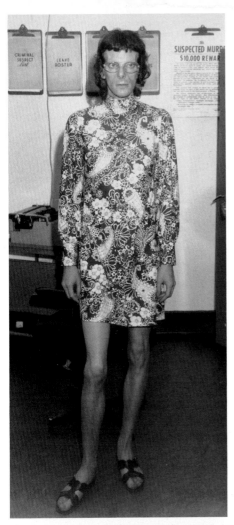

Left: Eugene Francis Jeffers in Cronulla Police Station.

Below: John Little's Toyota parked outside the halfway house in Darlinghurst.

AT MT SUGARLOAF

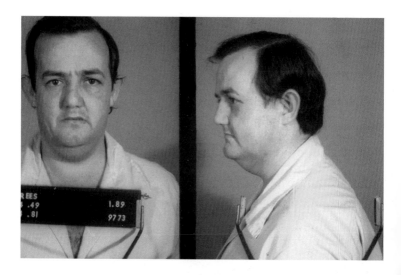

SUSPECTED MURDER
$5,000 REWARD

AT about 7.30p.m. on Sunday, the 25th June, 1967, Richard Gabriel Reilly, aged 58 years, was shot and killed in Manning Road, Double Bay. The post-mortem examination disclosed that death was due to a bullet wound in the neck. There were a number of other wounds found on the body which were caused by pellets discharged from a shotgun.

Notice is hereby given that a reward of five thousand dollars ($5,000) will be paid by the Government of New South Wales for such information as will lead to the arrest of the person or persons responsible for the death of Richard Gabriel Reilly. In addition, His Excellency the Governor will be advised to extend a free pardon to any accomplice, not being the person who actually committed the crime, who first gives such information.

This reward will remain in force for a period of 12 months from the date of this notice and its allocation will be at the sole discretion of the Commissioner of Police.

The co-operation and assistance of all members of the public is urgently sought in this matter. Any information, which will be treated as confidential, may be given at any time of the day or night by telephoning:

Police Emergency, 2222;
Police Communications Centre, 2 0966;
Reception Officer, Criminal Investigation Branch, 2 0966,
extension 3162;

or any police station.

Premiers Department   R.W. Askin,
Sydney, 3rd January, 1968.   Premier.

813 1.68   SYDNEY: V.C.N. BLIGHT, GOVERNMENT PRINTER-1968

Opposite top: Police examine the scene around Rees' Valiant where Constable Alexander Pietruska was shot down.

Opposite bottom: Front and profile shots of Berwyn Rees at his arrest.

Above: The lounge room of 17/189 President Ave, Kogarah, showing the bloodstain on the carpet next to John Warren's gun.

Left: Reward poster for information leading to the arrest of the person or persons responsible for the death of Richard Gabriel Reilly.

Constable McQueen
1.6.62–5.5.89

Constable Forsyth
15.5.69–27.2.98

Constable Carty
15.11.71–18.4.99

Snr Constable Affleck
9.7.57–14.1.01

Snr Constable Thornton
28.4.66–13.4.02

Snr Constable McEnallay
10.3.76–3.4.02

NSW Police officers killed in the line of duty.

Towers. The task of solving that explosion was now doubled. There could be little doubt that both offences were related as the Hakoah Club was controlled and operated by Jews.

THE INVESTIGATION

A task force of 80 personnel was established to inquire into both attacks and I was placed in command. Known simply as the Bomb Task Force, we were located in the Emergency Room of the State Intelligence Building in Surry Hills. The room had everything: telephones, typewriters, police radio receivers, transmitters, blackboards, whiteboards, drawing boards and a library of law books and crime manuals.

NSW Police formed the bulk of the task force, complemented by Federal Police officers to inquire into passport-related inquiries and immigration movements. Australian Security Intelligence Organisation agents were selected for their ability to infiltrate criminal organisations. Trained criminal analysts would be used to piece together the jigsaw of names and associations of persons involved, with a visual, operational link chart.

A media liaison officer was essential to issue press releases. Police scientists were already in the investigation, using their specialised skills in examining exhibits taken from the crime scenes. The clerks filed and indexed all information received and the operational investigators who gathered that information completed the team.

A single car registration numberplate remained on the front of the damaged Valiant. The registered owner was promptly visited at her home in Kogarah, in southern

Sydney. She informed investigators that her car had been stolen on 20 December and had been recovered at Greenacre in the west, minus the numberplates. The theft had been reported to police, this being confirmed by the task force. This information also created a veil of doubt to an inquiring mind. If the numberplates were all that were wanted, why not just steal them and not run the risk of being caught in a stolen car?

The engine number of the Valiant was lifted in an etching examination by police scientists. Records at the Roads and Traffic Authority (RTA) showed that the car was registered to Grenadier Motors, a car sales yard at 432 Parramatta Road, Burwood.

The two police officers hid their excitement as they spoke to David Hawthorne, the car yard owner. He had sold the car on 14 December 1982, but had not yet registered the transfer with the RTA. His sales book showed the purchase was made by David Hoffman of 27 Kelsey Road, Bondi. Hoffman was described as being in his early thirties, of solid build and Arabic appearance. The officers' elation turned to frustration when inquiries revealed that both the name Hoffman and the Bondi address were fictitious.

The LP gas cylinders had been ruptured in the Hakoah Club explosion, but the collar of one had been recovered in the debris. The serial number remained visible on the exhibit. The manufacturer was Rheem Australia Ltd in the northwestern suburb of Rydalmere. The company kept accurate records of the placement of their products and were able to tell the task force that the cylinder from the bombing had been allocated to the NSW State Rail Authority two years earlier.

State Rail used the cylinders to power the luggage trolleys about the country and interstate passenger platforms at Central Railway Station. There were 23 platforms, each leading to a grand terminal and the luggage collection area. The trolleys wound like snakes to the area with their variety of baggage. The last recorded movement of the cylinder listed on rail inventory showed that it was placed in the storage compound of the nearby Redfern workshops.

The owner of the stolen car registration plates continued to rouse the interest of investigators and her background was checked. She had migrated from Lebanon to Sydney with her parents and brother in the 1970s. Her parents were elderly and her brother was 33 years old. What was his background?

His name was Mohammed Beshwan. He had been born in the town of Bint Ibeil in Lebanon, and was obviously an intelligent person. As an adult, Beshwan took up a position as a schoolteacher in the country town of Froun. He tired of the profession and became a security guard at the parliamentary building in Beirut, where he gained knowledge of both security enforcement and evasion. Beshwan lived with his wife at Ramsgate to the south of Sydney.

Beshwan was placed under surveillance. He led an undercover Observation Squad member to the overseas terminal of the international airport at Mascot, where it was established he worked as a mail sorter for Australia Post whose office was on the first level. His description was of interest. He was solidly built and of obvious Arabic appearance.

Arrangements were made for David Hawthorne to make observations at the airport in an endeavour to identify Beshwan as the purchaser of the Valiant car. At 6am on

28 January 1983, Hawthorne was conveyed by police to the overseas passenger terminal. Conditions were ideal for the task of an identification. Several early morning flights were discharging their passengers into the terminal. Hawthorne and plainclothes police mixed in with the crowd of relatives and friends greeting the arrivals.

Hawthorne looked intently at the multitude of faces passing him. The terminal clock had just reached 07.10 hours when he said, 'That's him. The bloke in the grey suit.'

Mohammed Beshwan had just entered the passenger lounge wearing a grey suit. He used the escalator to go to the first floor. Hawthorne had identified the man who had purchased the Valiant sedan, later to be used as a car bomb.

On 1 February 1983, Beshwan was arrested at his home. When interviewed regarding the bombing offence, he denied any involvement, similarly denying that he had purchased the car from David Hawthorne. The car salesman's identification was strong and, relying on this evidence, Beshwan was charged with being an accessory before the fact of the bombing of the Hakoah Club, by a person unknown. He was remanded and released on bail of $200,000. Despite this arrest, the inquiry was still very much open.

A CONNECTION

The Hakoah Club already had yielded evidence and exhibits of great importance. Another was to emerge.

The timing device used in the explosion had been recovered almost intact. Scientists closely examined this unfamiliar piece. Their conclusion was that the casing was of an epoxy resin material in the shape and size of a matchbox. A wiring circuit had been pressed inside the circuit with a wire protruding from each end of the device. The circuit was interrupted by a Plessey brand E-cell resistor. One wire was attached to a battery power pack, the other to a spent detonator. When the life of the E-cell had eroded after the continuing battery surge, it would break down, completing the circuit and allowing the power to proceed to the detonator, setting off the explosion.

In March 1983, an International Air Security Summit was hosted by the Australian airline Qantas at their Sydney base. Trevor Chaseling was the head of Qantas security and a former NSW Police officer. He came to the task force office and introduced me to Paul Lavinski from New York City, the officer in charge of the security portfolio for Pan American World Airways. This American airline service was owned by the USA Bankers and Trust Company. Before taking up the position, Lavinski had worked as a special agent with the Federal Bureau of Investigation (FBI). The American showed particular interest in the two Sydney bombings, especially the construction of the recovered timing device.

He expressed an opinion that the device was similar to ones being held in the FBI laboratory in Washington DC. Lavinski outlined a story that well and truly could connect Australia to other, international terrorist activity.

On 11 August 1982, just four months prior to the Sydney explosions, Pan American Airways flight 830 left Narita, Japan, en route to Honolulu. While the plane was in flight, a bomb exploded under the cushion of seat 47K, killing

Tora Ozawa, a 14-year-old Japanese youth. The aircraft was damaged but able to be piloted on to Honolulu, where it made an emergency landing. Over 70 exhibits were taken from the aircraft by FBI agents, including an epoxy resin-cased timing device. Two weeks later, on 25 August 1982, an unexploded bomb was found on Pan American Airways flight N748, while it was being cleaned at Rio de Janeiro airport in Brazil. Another similar timing device was located, attached to the explosive material. The speculation from Lavinski that the two timing devices were similar to ours encouraged me to obtain government authority to travel to Washington to compare the Hakoah Club device with those in possession of the FBI.

On 8 May I arrived in Washington and went directly to the FBI headquarters in the J Edgar Hoover Building. There, X-rays were taken of the device in the Explosives Unit. Laser examinations were made and samples snipped from resin, wiring and cord binding for comparison with the American devices. Stuart Case was the senior explosives agent and his conclusions were recorded in his official report.

Technical analysis has proven that the PETN/LATEX material is the simplest and crudest military raw grade explosive. That which was recovered in Rio de Janeiro is of the same type and composition and also from the same batch as that recovered in Honolulu. Fragments of wire, string, tape, metal and potting material taken from the Sydney device are identical with the Honolulu and Rio de Janeiro devices. As the device from Brazil was recovered intact, the design has been established...

The timing/detonation components included a Plessey Electro Products series 560 item, referred to as an E Cell, one resistor, a silicon control rectifier and an electric blasting cap. An improvised pressure switch was included in the circuitry between the E Cell and a battery pack consisting of two, triple A batteries. The batteries were bound together by a black plastic tape, forming a three volt power pack. This was then connected to a battery plug which mated with the timing detonation device.

When pressure was applied to the device, such as someone sitting in the seat, the power would flow from the E Cell until it expended and the circuit would connect causing detonation. E Cells can be charged with different life expectancies, in the case of the Rio de Janeiro device, a further two hours of life existed with the consistent or concurrent connection.

The PETN was white to grey in colour and was cut to fit into a briefcase for later removal and placement under the aircraft seat cushion. The explosive sheets contained a honeycomb mesh netting, similar to cheese cloth which was moulded into the sheet during manufacture.

There can be no doubt that the Honolulu, Rio de Janeiro and the Sydney device, came from the same source.

Before leaving Washington, I was given unconfirmed information that a member of the 15 May terrorist group had just been detained in Berne, Switzerland, in possession of similar timing detonation devices. He was cooperating with FBI agents in exchange for protection. Information, to that time, was that the devices had been manufactured in Baghdad, and couriers were delivering them around the world. Sydney had been mentioned as one delivery point.

With this knowledge, plus the results of the timing device examination, a possible Sydney scenario was fashioned that a 15 May courier had travelled to Sydney and remained in the transit lounge of the airline company within the international terminal. His immigration papers would not have shown him as disembarking in Sydney as he would rejoin the plane and travel further. He could be met in the transit lounge by an accomplice based in Sydney, a 'sleeper' who had security clearance and access to restricted areas in the airport. The timing device could be passed to this person. The question was, could the accomplice be a postal worker who had such clearances?

While no direct evidence had been gained to support this theory, the supposition remained

A SUSPECT IS ARRESTED

On 16 December 1983, Mohammed Beshwan appeared at the Central Court of Petty Sessions where evidence was taken, including the report from FBI agent Stuart Case. A prima facie case against the defendant was made out. The matter, however, proceeded no further as the main witness for the prosecution, David Hawthorne, had left Australia and the case could not be successfully brought to trial without his evidence.

On 15 January 1987, a grand jury was sworn in at the United States District Court for the District of Columbia. Indictments were filed against Abu Ibraham, Mohammed Rashed and Christine Pinter, in their absence. The indictments related to their involvement with the 15 May terrorist group responsible for murder and aircraft sabotage of Pan American Airways aircraft. The terrorist who had been detained in Switzerland gave evidence, and is now in strict, protective custody.

Available evidence indicates 15 May were involved in the Sydney bombings of December 1982, and proof may lie with the three grand jury defendants and the informant. Interviews with one, or all, of those individuals is not possible until the conclusion of the United States legal proceedings. As at early 1998, each defendant remained at large, outside the United States.

In July 1998, seven years after my retirement from the NSW Police Force, I heard a snippet of news in a news bulletin broadcast over a Sydney commercial radio station. It was ever so short, but ever so important: 'FBI agents today extradited to America from Germany Mohammed Rashed, involved in the bombing of a Pan Am jet in 1982 when a young Japanese passenger was killed.'

In police parlance, 'Inquiries are continuing'.

CHAPTER SIX

MURDER NEVER CHANGES

In 1974, a murder took place at Kurnell, the birthplace of Australia. The computer age has since arrived and the manner in which police now store and accumulate information and evidence has changed beyond my expectations when I investigated this particular case. However, the manner in which police gather evidence remains very much the same as it did then: by intuition, canvassing, communication and cooperation.

Inscribed on a wall at the entrance to the Federal Bureau of Investigation building in Washington DC are the words: 'The most effective weapon against crime is cooperation.' Many law enforcement agencies have an intelligence branch. Much of that knowledge is received, indexed, filed and kept as an information bank. With proper communication it could be handed to operatives to investigate before gathering dust.

THE CRIME

Richard Francis Gannon was born in Victoria in 1944. In 1964, when Richard was 20 years old, the feminine side of him became overwhelming. He changed his name by deed poll to Eugene Francis Jeffers and began dressing and living as a woman. Jeffers then moved to Sydney and established herself in the Kings Cross area.

Jeffers became well known as a trustworthy babysitter to the children of prostitutes. She lived in backpacker-style accommodation, sharing a room at 249 Forbes Street, Darlinghurst. She was 30 years old when she decided on a different lifestyle, that of a live-in housekeeper.

On Tuesday 5 November 1974, Eugene went to the Community Contact Centre in Cronulla, a southern beach suburb of Sydney. The centre was conducted by the NSW Health Department and an appointment had been made by Jeffers for an interview with a social worker.

Jean, as she liked to be called, dressed carefully for the interview. She wore pink slacks, a white blouse, sandals and cheap plastic jewellery. Standing at 182 centimetres tall, Jeffers was very thin with pale skin and a deep and manly voice. She may have given the outward impression of being a woman, but a very unattractive one. The social worker was aware that Jean was a male, but disregarded this fact as being unimportant when assessing her for live-in employment, preferably caring for an elderly male pensioner.

John Albert Little was a 72-year-old invalid pensioner who lived alone in his small home at 102 Bridges Street, Kurnell, about seven kilometres from Cronulla. He had applied for a live-in housekeeper to help him with his daily chores and had left his details with the Community Contact Centre.

The old man was partially blind and unable to walk without the aid of a crutch. He could, however, drive a car and his pride and joy was a white 1970 Toyota station wagon, purchased with funds he had received as part of an insurance payout following a car accident. Little had been widowed for 30 years and had lived in his Kurnell home for 15 years. He was well known and liked in his small village neighbourhood.

The social worker arranged a further meeting for the following day, 6 November. At the meeting Jeffers was offered the position by John Little, who was ignorant of the fact that his new housekeeper was a man. To all intents and purposes, he had just employed a 30-year-old woman.

The unlikely pair left the centre and drove in Little's Toyota to the modest, three-bedroom brick-clad home at Kurnell. Jeffers was allocated a bedroom and she immediately set about making herself at home.

That first night, Jeffers cooked a simple meal of sausages and vegetables, after which she and Little settled in to watch television. At 9.30pm, they both retired to their respective bedrooms for the evening.

The following morning, Thursday 7 November, after cooking breakfast, Jeffers was set a number of tasks by Little: shopping, cleaning, gardening and more cooking. It became obvious to Jeffers that this was not an easy, simple meal ticket. Her frail body soon began to feel the strain of these unaccustomed domestic duties and cracks began to appear in the new relationship.

The housekeeper and her elderly employer argued on the next morning, Friday 8 November, when Little accused

Jeffers of being lazy and staying in bed too long. A trip into Cronulla had already been planned for the reluctant housekeeper, this time to withdraw money from a Commonwealth Bank account kept by Little. A withdrawal slip for $12 was signed and the passbook handed over to Jeffers, who set off complaining.

Jeffers checked the passbook and was surprised to discover that the old man had several thousand dollars in savings. A scheme began to develop in her mind. She carefully traced the old man's signature from the withdrawal slip onto a piece of paper, which she could then use later to withdraw money from the account. She returned to Kurnell, her mind busy with plans on how to capitalise on her possible, new-found source of wealth.

Later that afternoon, she and Little again argued heatedly. The pensioner accused his new employee of being lazy and of no comfort to him.

Jeffers had a short temper and was now furious. She went into the backyard of the house and picked up a length of hardwood from a pile of timber near the outhouse. She then walked into the lounge room where Little was sitting and shouted, 'Do you want me to do every fucking thing?'

The old man saw the blow coming and raised his wooden crutch in an effort to ward off the inevitable. He implored her, 'Don't be silly. Don't be silly.'

The length of hardwood struck a cruel blow on the old man's shoulder, knocking him to the floor. Stunned, he tried vainly to get to his feet, only to be felled by another savage strike, this time to his head. A frenzy of blows then rained down on Little's head, beating it to a pulp, Jeffers only stopping when she was satisfied that the old man was dead.

Unaffected by the killing, Jeffers calmly walked into her bedroom, packed her meagre belongings in a case, stole the victim's car and house keys and left the house. She locked the door behind her and took ownership of the old man's precious Toyota, setting off to her old refuge in Forbes Street in Darlinghurst.

The next morning, Jeffers met up with an acquaintance, 20-year-old New Zealander Neil Stephens. She was excited over what she had done and couldn't wait to confide to Stephens the gruesome details of the cold-blooded murder. She suggested that she and Stephens return to the dead man's house and steal any valuables they could find which they could later pawn for cash. She then mentioned the bank account from which she could withdraw the funds that would enable them both to travel in the stolen Toyota to Melbourne, where they could start a new life together.

Stephens readily agreed to the proposal and, later that evening, the pair returned to Kurnell in Little's car. They parked the vehicle away from the old man's house and approached on foot. The New Zealander took the house keys from Jeffers, told her to wait outside, and then went into the house to ensure that the victim was dead.

Stephens walked into the lounge room, found the light switch and turned on the lights. The body of John Little lay on the floor before him. The man's head was smashed in and he was lying in a dark pool of congealed blood. More blood was splattered all about the room. Stephens went into a bedroom and removed a pink bedspread which he used to cover the body.

He called to Jeffers to come into the house. The two then proceeded to ransack the home, stealing Little's few valuable possessions: a radio, an electric fan, binoculars, clothing and some food. They left the house in darkness, locking the front door behind them. The two partners in crime even stole the bottle of milk and newspaper from where they had been delivered on the front step.

Jeffers and Stephens returned to the city and later pawned the stolen property for $30. The pair planned to steal another vehicle's registration plates to replace those on Little's Toyota, thinking that this would enable them to avoid detection when his body and the theft of the car were eventually discovered.

As yet, there were no solid plans for travelling to Melbourne. The couple decided to remain at the halfway house, at least for the time being.

THE DISCOVERY

On Tuesday 12 November 1974, some four days after the murder, Mrs Vickery, an immediate neighbour of the victim, took her daily walk past his home. Her sharp eyes noticed that the milk and newspapers had been left on the front step of his house. She became concerned, realising that she had not seen her neighbour for several days.

Returning to her home, she rang James Little, the 58-year-old, younger brother of her neighbour. After hearing from Mrs Vickery, James Little also became concerned about his brother's welfare. He drove from his home at Kogarah, arriving at Kurnell 20 minutes later, at 6pm.

He entered the house through the rear door, using a key his brother had given to him. The late afternoon light filtered through the curtained windows, illuminating the murder scene. It was quite obvious to him that his brother had been dead for some time. James Little immediately phoned the police.

The call came through to my partner and I at Cronulla Police Station. A systematic procedure followed, as in all murder investigations. The crime scene, the house, was secured and isolated. Scientific police experts documented all evidence and the government forensic pathologist coaxed clues from the battered corpse.

When these examinations were completed, arrangements were made for the body to be conveyed to the city morgue, where a full post-mortem would be carried out to establish the time and cause of death. Detectives would witness this procedure as the pathologist revealed the secrets of the deceased.

At the crime scene our attention was focused on the problems ahead. Where did we start? What steps did we take? A canvass of homes in the close vicinity was made, and Mrs Vickery was the first to be interviewed. Police officers were pleased that she was a talkative woman with an inquiring mind. The information she recalled was to prove a great help in the investigation.

Mrs Vickery told detectives that over the years, the victim had employed a number of housekeepers. The most recent one, she said, was just 'plain ugly'. She was sure the person wore a wig, because she had seen it airing on the clothesline and it was similar to the housekeeper's hair.

Mrs Vickery's son Stephen had also paid close attention to the new housekeeper. He thought that her movements were 'masculine' and believed that the woman was in fact a male. Stephen remembered that during the evening of

Friday 8 November 1974, he had seen the housekeeper drive away from Mr Little's home in the white Toyota. She was alone in the car.

A check with the then Department of Motor Transport, now the Roads and Traffic Authority, established the registration plate of the missing car. A police wireless message was broadcast across the metropolitan area, alerting police to look out for the car, possibly in the possession of the transvestite housekeeper.

Mrs King, the immediate neighbour on the other side of Little's home, was interviewed. She was more sparing with her words, but what she did have to say was of utmost interest to the police. According to her, about 2.30pm on the afternoon of Friday 8 November, she and her husband heard banging noises coming from Mr Little's house. The noises were loud and strong enough to vibrate through the floor of the neighbouring home. Mrs King described the noise as sounding like someone hitting the floorboards with a heavy object. After a few seconds, the noises stopped and all was quiet. Although both she and Mr King thought the noises were unusual, they decided not to investigate.

Detectives worked through the night, submitting the reams of paperwork required in such an investigation. Running sheets were commenced, following up every scrap of information. The phones rang hot, either from people with something to report or senior police putting in their suggestions on how to conduct the inquiry. The media were also sniffing, hungry for anything to print.

A plan of action was developed. In those days, the detectives would hold 'scrum downs', which today are called problem-solving sessions to implement strategies to target and attain objectives to would achieve a goal. We had our 'scrum down'. While we were well under way with the inquiry, the offender was also busy.

TELLING SECRETS

Back at the halfway house in Darlinghurst, Jeffers sat down opposite the 'house leader', 37-year-old Elaine Payne. It was 7.30am on Wednesday 13 November, five days after the murder.

As they both enjoyed a morning cup of tea, Jeffers said to Payne, 'Can I trust you?'

'Yes, of course you can,' was Payne's reply, obviously interested in what secret Jeffers wanted to tell to her.

'Neil and I are going to Melbourne today in that white Toyota I've got. There's only one thing. The car's hot.'

Elaine Payne was more shocked than surprised. 'Well, you had better get it away from here and back to where it belongs,' she replied.

Jeffers whined, 'But I couldn't do that. It's too good to get rid of. We're going to get different numberplates for it. I may as well tell you the rest.'

If Payne was already shocked, she was about to experience a much greater trauma.

'I got this housekeeping job on Wednesday with an old man, Jack Little, at Kurnell. On Thursday we went to do some shopping and he sent me into the same shop eight times which made me mad and I knew then that I was going to kill him. On Friday afternoon, he told me to pack my bags and leave, but I had nowhere to go. Anyway, I had this piece of wood and he was coming down the hall towards me on his crutches. We were yelling at each other and then I hit him with the piece of wood and he fell back on the lounge. He hit me with his crutch. I don't know where, I was so mad, I didn't feel it. I just kept bashing into him.'

Elaine Payne couldn't believe what she was hearing. She was stunned at this unsolicited confession of murder. Then she managed to speak. 'Did you just leave him there?' she asked.

'Yes,' said Jeffers as she continued her story. 'I left the garage door up so it would look like we had gone out. I had some blood on the bottom of my slacks and feet, but they're alright now. I've washed them. Neil and I went over on Saturday night. Neil wouldn't let me go in before he covered him up with a blanket. We took the fan and the transistor radio and we hocked them on Monday. I let Neil have the money for the radio. You know, I might even become famous, like Ronald Biggs.'

Payne, still reeling from the shock of the revelation, excused herself under the pretence of visiting the local Smith Family charity shop. Once away from the refuge, she rushed to the nearest phone box and rang Darlinghurst Police Station.

Police went straight to the halfway house, where they found the stolen Toyota parked boldly, right out the front. Two detectives entered the house. Eugene Jeffers was sitting quietly at a table as the officers introduced themselves. Jeffers was cautioned that she need not say anything unless she wanted to, but she certainly did. She held nothing back.

'Why lie about it?' she said. 'I killed the old man. He was a nasty thing. He wanted me to do everything; his banking, even his gardening. He was such a nark and said that if he couldn't get a housekeeper to stay with him, he'd take an overdose of pills. I thought I'd save him the trouble and belted him over the head with a piece of wood. I took his car and was going to go to Melbourne in it. The only reason I'm still here is because I'm waiting for my pension cheque to come through.'

What Jeffers hadn't remembered was that she had supplied the Kurnell address to the pension authorities as her change of address. The police had taken possession of the cheque when it arrived at the victim's address. They realised the name on the cheque, Eugene F. Jeffers, was possibly the owner of the 'unattractive' face.

Neil Stephens was also at the halfway house when police arrived to interview Jeffers. He was spoken to and admitted his participation in the events following the murder.

Both offenders were taken to Cronulla Police Station, where they were interviewed by the investigating detectives. Neither Jeffers nor Stephens felt remorse for what they had done and readily admitted their role in the callous crimes committed against John Little.

Eugene Jeffers was charged with the murder of John Little. Neil Stephens was charged with being an accessory after the fact of murder, by maintaining, harbouring and assisting Jeffers. He was later to escape prosecution when the Attorney General's Department decided not to file a bill and the charge against him was dropped.

Late in 1975, Eugene Francis Jeffers appeared in the Central Criminal Court and was convicted of murder. She was sentenced to penal servitude for life.

The boastful and calculating nature of the offender resulted in a successful police investigation and prosecution but the old-fashioned methods of canvassing, communicating and cooperation had resulted in a positive identification of the offender. It would only have been a matter of time before the detectives' net closed in on Eugene Jeffers.

CHAPTER SEVEN
FRIENDS

Why are friendships formed? People enter relationships for a number of reasons. Companionship, brotherhood and good fellowship are but three. Paul Gerald Mason was different. He had psychopathic motives that enabled him to become close to his unsuspecting victims. Mason was a serial killer.

Paul Mason was born on 28 June 1961 in Sydney. He was single, unemployed and resided with his father at Riverstone, an outer western suburb of Sydney. He was a 'friend' of Grant and Mary Clark, who lived on the farming property 'Oakdale' in Gundaroo Road, Geary's Gap, about 30 kilometres north of Canberra.

That association originated through Mason's and Grant Clark's common interest in rock climbing. They met regularly to participate in their hobby. Mason was a constant visitor to the farm. On one occasion, he found himself alone with Mary and he made unwanted sexual advances towards her. He was swiftly rejected by his friend's wife, and when Grant returned home an argument between the two men followed.

Mason brooded for months over the incident and decided that he would try again—only this time he did not intend to fail. He devised a cruel plan to get his revenge by travelling to the isolated Oakdale property and sneaking into the house when the opportunity presented itself. He would kill Grant Clark and his baby son Samuel, then rape and kill Mary. Their bodies were to be buried in the surrounding bushland or left to be devoured by wild animals.

THE PAYBACK

On 11 May 1989, Mason boarded the midnight train from Central Railway Station in Sydney, bound for Canberra. He was an experienced bushman and walked from the nation's capital to the Clarks' farm, arriving at sunrise the following day. After hiding in a barn, he kept observations of the house and the movements of the occupants.

Mary Alice Clark was in her early twenties and ten weeks pregnant with her second child. She intended to spend the day preparing a birthday party for their son Samuel, who was one year old that day. After breakfast, Grant left the home to work on the land. Mason decided that now was the time to put his plan into action.

Before moving towards the house, Mason took possession of a mountain-climber's pickaxe that was hanging from a rack in the hayshed. He would deal with Mary and her son first and then wait for Grant to return.

Mary Clark had just placed Samuel in his cot for his morning nap and was in the process of cleaning up in the kitchen when she was grabbed from behind by Mason who had entered the house through an unlocked back door. He quickly bound her with rope and tape that he had brought with him and then gagged her with a tea towel to muffle her screams for help.

The offender carried her into a bedroom and tossed her onto a bed. Mary Clark was a fighter and struggled against Mason who was attempting to strip her clothing from her. Realising that a sexual conquest was out of the question, he decided to kill her.

Mason picked up the pickaxe and, with five sharp blows to her head, he delivered what later proved to be fatal injuries. He then went to Samuel's room and threw a heavy doona over the child, tucking it firmly around his head and leaving him to smother.

Having lost the urge to remain in the house and murder the victim's husband, Mason pulled the telephone cord from its socket and fled. As he left the Clarks' property he hid the murder weapon under shrubbery about 700 metres from the farmhouse. He then made his way back to his Riverstone home in Sydney, feeling no contrition for his crime.

Grant Clark returned to the farmhouse mid morning and was horrified to discover his wife trussed up and bleeding from head wounds. He heard a muffled cry coming from Samuel's bedroom and quickly uncovered the child.

Wasting little time, Clark drove his wife and son to Canberra Hospital. Samuel survived, but Mary was pronounced dead on arrival. Police were called and a murder investigation swung into action.

Suspicion inevitably rested upon the spouse, as so many murders are committed by a jealous or tormented partner.

A number of questions were put to Grant as a possible suspect. The real offender, however, was well away from the scene and had already prepared an alibi that he had been rock climbing in the Blue Mountains.

A post-mortem examination on the body of Mary Clark showed that she died as a result of brain injuries inflicted by a heavy, sharp implement. The murder weapon had not been found at the crime scene. Despite a thorough search, it could not be located.

The usual investigation by Homicide Squad took place—photographs were taken and the house was checked for fingerprints. There were no immediate neighbours to interview as the property was isolated. Press releases were made seeking public assistance, but nothing of help came from them. Another tragedy would occur before the investigators focused their attention on Paul Mason.

ANOTHER 'FRIEND'

On the evening of 27 July 1989, a young detective from the NSW south coast town of Bega phoned me at my home. He asked for my assistance at the scene of a murder at nearby Pambula Beach.

The Police Air Wing provided a small aircraft to take me to the airport at Merimbula. There I was met by local police who drove me to Calgoa Crescent in Pambula Beach. Parked in an open, double garage of a neat house was a Sigma sedan with the luggage compartment open.

Inside that boot was a sickening sight: the semi-naked body of a young adult woman, her feet and wrists bound with rope, and lying next to her, the body of a baby boy with a length of rope and a baby's bib fastened tightly around his neck. Next to the bodies was a bloodied, mountain climber's pickaxe.

The circumstances surrounding the deaths began to unfold. Ruth Margaret Ferguson was 25 years old and lived with her husband Greg and their eight-month-old son Mark in the Pambula Beach cottage. Ruth had been a school friend of Paul Mason and his sister had been a bridesmaid at Ruth and Greg's wedding.

Paul Mason's father owned a cottage at Eden, which was not too far from Pambula Beach and Paul had been visiting there in July 1989. Prior to leaving Sydney, Mason had gone to a camping equipment store in the city and purchased a mountain climber's pickaxe. He packed it in a large sports bag, along with ropes, tapes, knives, a bow and arrows, as well as a .303 calibre rifle. Such items suggested he meant to embark on a hunting trip. He did, but the game was human.

At 8.30am on 27 July 1989, two months after the murder of Mary Clark, the hunter arrived unexpectedly at the Fergusons' home. His arrival was well planned and timed. Greetings were exchanged as he was accepted as a friend. Greg Ferguson was a schoolteacher and was just about to leave for work. Having no undue concern for his family's safety, he left his wife and baby alone with Mason. On his return that evening, Greg was confronted with the horrific sight of his family, murdered.

After speaking with the distraught husband, police had no doubt that Paul Mason was the offender. Moreover, the similarity of the pickaxe slaying of Mary Clark, who had also been a friend of the suspect, linked him unquestionably to both crimes.

From information supplied by Greg Ferguson, police knew that Mason had left the scene of the murders in his sister's car. A description of the vehicle was broadcast over the police radio network.

THE MANHUNT

A suspect's MO (modus operandi or mode of behaviour) is an important element in police investigations. A study of a criminal's MO can often predict what action he or she might take after committing an offence. Mason was no exception and his behaviour was not surprising.

He left Pambula Beach at 3pm and drove back to where the killings first started, at the Clarks' Oakdale property. He bought petrol for the vehicle en route, with money he had stolen from his latest victim.

In the dense bushland around the property Mason felt safe, but when the car became bogged he was left to escape the law on foot. A massive search centred around the property following the discovery of his abandoned vehicle, but he was not sighted again until he surrendered to the Woden Police in Canberra, two days later.

NSW detectives investigating the murders of Mary Clark and Ruth and Mark Ferguson interviewed Mason, who displayed a trait so often found in serial killers, that of selfishness in place of remorse—he wanted a meal. The purse he had stolen from Mrs Ferguson's home, minus the contents, was still in his possession and was taken as an exhibit.

Mason was driven by police to the Clarks' Oakdale property, where he indicated the location of the hidden pickaxe. Daylight was fading so police used the services of a light aircraft to fly Mason to Pambula Beach, where he re-enacted his movements on the day of Ruth and Mark Ferguson's murders.

When Paul Mason was asked why he committed these terrible crimes, his simple reply was, 'A thrill kill I suppose—for enjoyment'.

THE CONFESSION

Mason was returned to Queanbeyan Police Station, where he participated in a recorded interview in relation to each crime. The murder of Mary Clark and the attempted murder of her son were as portrayed earlier in this story. The inhumanity of Ruth and Mark Ferguson's murders can only be explained by extracts from the recorded interview.

> Mason (hereafter 'A'): I gave myself up for the murder of Ruth, Mark and Mary—that is Ruth Margaret Ferguson, Mark Ferguson and Mary Alice Clark.

> Q: Can you tell me how you killed Ruth Ferguson?

> A: With an ice axe, hitting her in the head with the pick. Repeatedly in the head, I suppose—I left it in the boot of the car—it was short handled, approximately 45 centimetre shaft with adze and pick on the head. The make is Laprade.

Q: Can you tell me how you killed the baby Mark Ferguson?

A: I strangled the baby with my hands, but the baby kept wanting to recover when I let go, so I had to tighten the bib around the baby's throat. This still did not work properly so I got the thicker rope from the lounge room which I had brought in from the car and tied that around the baby's throat.

Q: Can you tell me what happened after you arrived at this address?

A: I left Eden about 8am that morning after one beer. I arrived at the Fergusons' about twenty past nine. I went up and rang the doorbell, taking a small day pack with me. Ruth answered the door and I walked in as Ruth's husband left for work. I went upstairs with Ruth. We talked for about an hour, looked at photo albums, then Ruth went to the kitchen to make something up in her blender. While she was there, I came up behind her with the sheaf knife that I had in my day pack, put it to her throat and told her to go into the hall and lay down where I pulled some cord from my pocket and bound her hands—I taped up her mouth and tied up her legs—the baby made loud noises so I strangled it.

Q: What happened then?

A: I raped her—carried her down to the car, her car, went and got the ice axe—then hit her repeatedly with the ice axe in the head. I went upstairs and got Mark and put him in the boot too and closed it.

Q: Can you tell me what conversation you had with Ruth Ferguson that day?

A: When I put the knife at her throat, I said, 'This is a very sharp knife, I'm serious.' Before I had sex with her she said, 'Don't Paul. You haven't done anything wrong yet, just leave now and everything will be alright.' I took my pants off and had sex with her. I told her, 'I'm just going to put you in the boot of the car, I'll bring Mark down in a moment.' I then got the ice axe and killed her.

Q: Can you tell me when you decided to kill Ruth Ferguson?

A: About two weeks beforehand. I knew she would be at home by herself after Greg went to work. It was the same as the first time, I got the urge to kill again.

Q: Apart from the injuries inflicted upon Ruth Ferguson which were caused by your ice axe, did you inflict any other injuries to her?

A: Yes—there might be some rope burns on limbs from where I tied her up. She could have bruising on one of her arms because she got the rope off and ran down the hall and ran into a wall fairly heavily. There could be other scratches and bruises because when I put her in the boot, I did it pretty roughly.

Q: Do you recall how many time you struck her with the ice axe?

A: In the dark I think I probably hit her several times, there could have been more glancing to her head. I tried to do it quickly and put as much force as possible into each blow to end it as quick as possible, but she kept screaming during the first few and when I stopped hitting her, she gave one more moan and was quiet.

The interview continued on for fifteen pages and it was difficult to treat Mason with the respect he had not shown to his victims.

On 30 July 1989, Mason was charged at Queanbeyan Police Station with three counts of murder and one of attempted murder. He was kept in custody, bail being refused.

At a press conference held on the steps of Queanbeyan Police Station, a detective, answering a question put to him by the media said, 'He's admitted to the murder of Mary Clark, Ruth Ferguson and Mark Ferguson'. This simple, true statement would have serious ramifications later, as the offender had not yet appeared in court.

After his eventual appearance in court, Mason was held in custody at Goulburn Jail in strict protection and separated from other prisoners. These steps to protect Mason were necessary as child killers are often subjected to physical abuse by their fellow inmates—an unwritten punishment for harming an innocent child.

As it turned out, however, it was not the criminal element that posed the main threat to Mason's health. At 7.07am on 11 September 1989, prison officers found Paul Gerald

Mason hanging in his cell. His lifeless body hung from a makeshift rope he had spliced together from torn up bed sheets. There was nothing suspicious about the circumstances of his death. Mason had taken the coward's way out and committed suicide.

THE CORONER'S FINDING

A Coronial Inquest into the deaths of the two women and the baby boy was conducted by the then State Coroner, Mr Kevin Waller. He sympathised with the relatives of the deceased who had gone through a terrible period. The coroner then found that each victim had died of the effects of injuries delivered by Paul Mason, since deceased. Mason had finally been found guilty.

An interesting comment was made by the coroner: 'It may be of interest in any later studies that some persons might do into the lives of multiple killers in Australia, that Mason has never expressed sorrow for his victims or their families. He has expressed regret for the situation in which he at last found himself—jail. But I've never heard anything given that he ever expressed a single word of sorrow for Mary Clark, Ruth Ferguson or Mark Ferguson or the devastation that he's caused to the families of those people.'

In regard to the murder of Mary Clark Mr Waller added that 'despite Mason saying he intended to kill the whole family, including Grant, he was apparently afraid to confront a man with such violence'.

The investigation into the brutal murders was complete. The case was closed. But not so for the media or the detective who uttered that statement on the steps of Queanbeyan Police Station following Mason's arrest.

On 11 October 1990, Detective Sergeant Len Dean appeared before Their Honours Gleeson, Kirby and Priestley in the Supreme Court of NSW charged with contempt. Standing alongside him was his co-opponent, the Amalgamated Television Services Pty Ltd. The claimant was the NSW Attorney General. The contempt was committed by the television company photographing Mason with the police during their reconstruction at the scenes of each murder and the publication of the detective's statement.

Consideration to the long, uninterrupted hours of duty performed by the police officer was given by the court and he was admonished without further penalty. The television company was not so fortunate and was fined $200,000 for 'broadcasting on television on 30th July 1989 matter which was likely or calculated or had a tendency to interfere with the administration of justice in connection with the trial of Paul Gerald Mason on three charges of murder and one charge of attempted murder'.

Several weeks later, Detective Sergeant Len Dean, who had worked so tirelessly and enthusiastically on the Mason murders inquiry, died suddenly from a heart attack. The long hours of duty and the consequences of his seemingly innocent statement had aggravated his condition. His loss was felt by many. Len Dean was my friend. He was up there with my best friends. Being so helpful and likeable, he would be accepted by those who met him as a true friend— except by the crooks.

CHAPTER EIGHT

THE FLYPAPER POISONINGS

My dear Watson, arsenic can also be obtained from boiling flypaper or even wallpaper.

Sherlock Holmes, in 'The Doctor'

In June 2002 I was visiting a relative at an aged care facility located in Newtown, an inner Sydney suburb. I was approached by another resident who was in his eighties. When he discovered that I was a retired police officer, his eyes began to sparkle.

'Have you solved many murders?' he asked me.

'A couple,' I replied.

'Do you remember the flypaper poisonings?' he queried.

'No. How long ago did it happen?' I asked.

'About sixty years ago. Before your time. It all happened near here. In St Mary Street. A woman named Coleman.'

When I finished my visit at the facility, my curiosity took charge. Back in my car, I reached for the street directory, located St Mary Street in Camperdown, and drove the short distance to the street. I had begun a search sparked by an old man's remark about 'flypaper poisonings'. I could remember that at the time to which the elderly man referred, people hung coils of flypaper from the ceilings of their homes to attract flies and trap them in a sticky substance, sealing their fate.

St Mary Street was crowded with semi-detached houses of the 1930s. It didn't prove a difficult task to locate the former home of Marjorie Coleman in such a small street. The older residents remembered the scandal. Apparently she first resided at number 42 but later moved two doors away, to number 38.

Marjorie Coleman was born on 30 September 1904 and was described by people who knew her as of medium build with brown hair and brown eyes. She was married, but her husband Charlie spent more time away than he did at home.

BOARDER TAKES ILL

On 12 July 1945, Constable William Patrick O'Dea, a member of the NSW Police Force went to board with Mrs Coleman at her home, which was then at 38 St Mary Street, Camperdown. O'Dea's marriage to his wife Violet had failed, and he moved out of their house in Wolsely Street, Bexley, a southern Sydney suburb.

He paid board of £2 a week to Marjorie Coleman, did odd jobs about the house and was reasonably content with his new lifestyle. That was until 21 January 1946, when he became violently ill after drinking a cup of tea that had been prepared for him by Marjorie Coleman. The following morning he again became terribly ill, again after drinking a cup of tea given to him by Mrs Coleman.

O'Dea attended Balmain Hospital, where he was admitted suffering from the loss of use of his limbs. He remained in the hospital until he was discharged almost two months later, on 23 March 1946. The constable returned to the boarding house in St Mary Street, but his illness returned two weeks later.

The police officer recalled that most of his food and drink was prepared for him by Mrs Coleman. On one occasion, he remarked to her that a glass of water was discoloured and had a bad taste. She replied that the water was alright, maybe it was from dirty waterpipes and his taste must have been affected by his illness.

Constable O'Dea also recalled mentioning to her in a conversation before he fell ill that he was expecting to inherit a legacy, although he had not given any further details of how much or from where it would originate. O'Dea had not himself made a will and was advised to do so by Mrs Coleman. She and her brother were to be the beneficiaries.

O'Dea's illness continued and, during September, he visited Dr Potts, a local physician. Dr Potts took hair samples and toenail and fingernail clippings and made a detailed examination. The results were incredible—O'Dea was being poisoned with arsenic.

The diagnosis gave the victim more reason to reflect on the 12-month period he had boarded with Mrs Coleman. He had been healthy when he moved in and had given no one, particularly Mrs Coleman, any reason to want to poison him. He was not her lover, although he would later say in a court hearing, 'I did take a cottage with her for a month at Tuggerah. I thought she was divorced, although I never exercised a husband's rights while we were away.'

Jealousy could not be a motive. If Coleman was the poisoner, was it because of O'Dea's will? O'Dea's thoughts became more intense as he concentrated on prior conversations and events.

Marjorie Coleman had once referred to an association she had with a man named Bob. He had 'done the dirty' on her and he subsequently died of pneumonia, brought about by self-administered poisoning. Bob had left a will in Coleman's favour, but she did not comment further as to its validity or execution.

As police delved into the circumstances surrounding the poisoning allegations made by O'Dea, a red herring concerning another poisoning attempt emerged, only this time the allegation was made by Coleman.

Mrs Coleman was employed by Irene Gladys Crocker as a cook at the Buxton Private Hospital. In September 1946, Coleman took ten days' absence on sick leave. The dates coincided with the same period as O'Dea's discovery that he was being poisoned.

When Mrs Coleman returned to her job, she told Mrs Crocker that O'Dea had attempted to poison her by soaking flypaper hangers in water, boiling them and obtaining a residue of arsenic. This he then placed in her food.

Had Marjorie Coleman given herself away by making this false claim and exposing her method of attempting to murder Constable O'Dea? In the meantime, the police officer had suffered enough and left the Camperdown address. The poisoning allegations would now be investigated by detectives from Sydney's Criminal Investigation Branch (CIB).

THE SECOND VICTIM

As the police investigation proceeded into the background of Marjorie Coleman, positive results began to appear. Between May and June 1946, Muriel Bewhey, a 26-year-old kitchenhand employed at Anzac House, Sydney, was also a boarder at Mrs Coleman's home. This was during the period when Constable O'Dea was a resident there.

Bewhey was a healthy woman, fond of her work with interests in dancing and surfing. On the evening of 16 May, Muriel went dancing with friends. The following morning, she drank a cup of tea prepared for her by Mrs Coleman. The tea tasted awful and she became suddenly ill. She left for work, still feeling queasy but on the way she became worse and returned to the Coleman house where she retired to bed. Unable to eat, Bewhey remained bedridden for four days.

'I felt as if I had no legs,' she said. 'I put on my cardigan, but could not feel my fingers doing up the buttons. I thought I must have been imagining things. When I started to drink, everything had a musty flavour.'

Muriel Bewhey's health deteriorated to such an extent that she was admitted to the Llandover Convalescent Home, in Hastings Road, Marrickville, where she was unable to walk without the assistance of leg braces.

Tests carried out on Bewhey revealed that she too was suffering from arsenic poisoning. This matter was also referred to the police. The report found its way to the desk of Detective Sergeant White at the CIB.

On 12 September 1946, Detectives Whites and Ferguson called at 38 St Mary Street. Marjorie Coleman answered the door.

'I know what you've come for,' she said by way of greeting the police officers. 'I won't answer any questions. I have nothing to say and I don't want to talk to you. Get away from the house.'

The detectives persisted. 'We have come to see you in connection with the illness of Miss Bewhey and Constable O'Dea. Can you give us any assistance in the matter?' Sergeant White asked her.

'What can I say about it?' replied Mrs Coleman. 'The doctors say that Muriel is poisoned and that it is probably from the asthma tablets.'

'What about Mr O'Dea?' was his next question.

'The doctor said he has anaemia and there is something the matter with his spinal cord,' she responded.

The officers searched the house, but no poisons were found.

'You won't find any poison. I don't keep any,' Coleman stated boldly.

It is, of course, not known what was in the minds of the investigators. Were they searching only for pure arsenic and not some other property from which the poison could be derived?

ANOTHER VICTIM

About this time, Constable O'Dea recalled what Mrs Coleman had said to him about the death of the man called

Bob. Investigations revealed that Bob was in fact Robert Walter Reynolds who was born in 1894 and worked as a truck driver for North Sydney Council. A married man, Robert had lived with his wife in Clark Street, Crows Nest. When Mrs Reynolds was interviewed she claimed that she and her husband were apparently happy and not an angry word had passed between them until, suddenly, on 27 June 1942, Robert left his wife and took up residence with Marjorie Coleman.

The live-in association did not last long. A few months later, a friend called Mrs Reynolds and delivered the short, sad message, 'Bob has passed away about 4.30 this afternoon in Camperdown'.

Dr Richard Speight of Annandale had been called to the boarding house to examine Robert Reynolds, who had been vomiting. In the opinion of the doctor, the patient was suffering from gastroenteritis and pneumonia. Arrangements were made to have Reynolds conveyed to hospital, but before this could be done, his condition deteriorated and he passed away.

Dr Speight issued a death certificate, thus no post-mortem examination was necessary or performed. The body of the deceased was buried at the Northern Suburbs Cemetery.

Robert Reynolds had made a will in favour of his wife about 13 years before his death. The will was contested by Mrs Coleman who stated that she was in possession of a later will. The Public Trustee, investigating the claim, asked Mrs Coleman to produce the final document. Not wishing to press her luck, she failed to do so and probate was granted to Mrs Reynolds.

In April 1943, Mrs Reynolds received an anonymous letter revealing that Marjorie Coleman had given birth to a daughter who was 'the living picture of Bob Reynolds'. This was in fact untrue. Someone was stirring the possum. The letter was forwarded to Detective Sergeant White at the CIB.

Questions evolved. Had Robert Reynolds died from poisoning and not as Dr Speight had certified? If so, was it self-administered? Marjorie Coleman was a common denominator and thus became a prime suspect.

Enough suspicion existed over Reynolds' death to warrant police seeking an exhumation order from the Sydney City Coroner. The application was successful and, on 24 October 1946, four years after his death, the remains of Robert Walter Reynolds were exhumed from his grave. Witnesses to this event were three NSW Police officers: Superintendent James, Detective Sergeant George White and Detective Don Ferguson.

An examination of the remains of the body was carried out by the government medical officer (GMO) and analyst of the day. The results were predictable: Robert Reynolds, for some time before his death, had been ingesting arsenic and that substance was still present in his remains, able to be detected by the GMO.

Police act initially on suspicion, followed by the gathering of evidence. The suspicion against Marjorie Coleman was that three persons who had boarded with her at her Camperdown homes had become seriously ill, and one of them had died. The three had suffered from arsenic poisoning, the toxin probably obtained by boiling flypaper traps in water and adding that liquid to the food and drink supplied to the victims.

Just who had administered that poison would remain for a court of law to decide.

On 9 November, detectives again visited Mrs Coleman. 'We have called to see you again in connection with the illness of Constable O'Dea and Miss Bewhey and the illness and death of Robert Reynolds in 1942,' Detective Sergeant White informed her.

Mrs Coleman remained steadfast. 'You can ask me any questions you like, but I do not have to answer and I am not going to make any statements.' Marjorie Coleman knew her rights and was going to exercise them.

The police believed they had sufficient evidence to mount a prima facie case against the woman. Mrs Coleman was arrested and taken to Central Police Station where she was charged with three charges of intent to murder Robert Walter Reynolds, William Patrick O'Dea and Muriel Jean Bewhey.

She was held in custody and remanded to appear at the Sydney City Coroners Court on 19 November 1946, when an inquest into the death of Robert Reynolds would be held. A leading lawyer at that time, Mr Jack Thom, was retained to represent and defend Mrs Coleman.

THE INQUEST

The Coronial Inquest began with the promise to be dramatic, sensational and full of suspense. Dr Speight gave evidence that when he attended Robert Reynolds in 1942, he diagnosed his patient was suffering from pneumonia and gastroenteritis. But now, taking everything into consideration, he would say death was consistent with arsenic poisoning. Under cross-examination from Mr Thom, the doctor also considered that death could be consistent with matters other than poisoning by arsenic.

The GMO, Dr Percy, supported by his junior, Dr Sheldon, told the coroner that although there was sufficient arsenic in Reynolds' body to have caused death, he did not think that he would be justified in saying that arsenic poisoning was the cause. He did not have sufficient knowledge of the deceased's prior health record to offer another possible reason.

The coroner then stated that 'as medical evidence could not give the exact cause of the death of Mr Reynolds, no good cause would be served by calling evidence which would not assist me in determining that cause.'

The only dramatic aspect of the inquest to arise was the suddenness of its conclusion. The coroner recorded an open finding. Marjorie Coleman remained in custody, awaiting committal proceedings at Central Court of Petty Sessions on the three charges of attempted murder.

During February 1947, a five-day hearing commenced at that court before Mr Hardwick, SM. Following evidence given by Constable O'Dea, Miss Bewhey and a variety of prosecution witnesses, the defendant was committed to stand trial at the Supreme Court on each of the three charges of attempted murder. Bail again was refused and Coleman remained behind bars.

An application was made by Mr Thom to the NSW Attorney General stating that the charges against his client lacked intensity. He claimed that any reasonable jury, properly instructed, would fail to convict. The Attorney General agreed and decided to not file a bill against Mrs Coleman. She was freed, and released from custody.

The case had now been finalised, but without a definitive result. It remained an enigma. Did she or didn't she kill Robert Reynolds? The suggestion raised by Marjorie Coleman that arsenic could be derived by soaking flypaper strips in boiling water intrigued me. Was it just an old wives' tale? Curious, I delved deeper into information on the substance.

ARSENIC AND ITS MISUSES

Arsenic, of course, is an element but it's also the common name for arsenic trioxide, a highly poisonous white powder compound. Its main use commercially is in the metallurgy industry for hardening of copper, lead and alloys. In the timber industry, it is used to treat timber and prevent rotting. Medically, the substance had been used to treat spirochetal infections, blood disorders, dermatitis and venereal disease. The symptoms of human toxicity are acute vomiting, abdominal pains, diarrhoea, convulsions, paralysis of limbs and anaemia, all common results of ingesting the poison.

In 1888, a case similar to the Coleman matter was prominent overseas. James and Florie Maybrick lived in the palatial Battlecrease House, Aigburth, in the United Kingdom. The marriage was not a happy one and, in March 1889, James became violently ill. His health deteriorated and, on 11 May, he died. Investigations showed that Florie had purchased a dozen flypapers from her chemist. It was alleged that she later obtained arsenic from those flypapers by boiling them in water and extracting the poison.

Other, similar cases are recorded. Eliza Barrow was

poisoned in London in the year 1911. On exhumation, her body was found to contain fatal amounts of arsenic, allegedly obtained by boiling flypapers.

In 1914, during World War I, in Nagyroo, Hungary, two midwives known later as 'the Angel Makers of Nagyroo', began boiling arsenic off flypapers to sell to women wishing to poison their husbands.

A general theory was established in the Victorian era that arsenic-impregnated flypaper was a common source of the poison. The musty taste of the substance could be disguised in brandy, coffee or tea.

THE ENIGMA

Following her release from custody in 1947, Marjorie Coleman moved from Camperdown. She was the talk of the neighbourhood, although she had not been found guilty of any crime. Suspicion was enough to condemn her. She moved to nearby Leichhardt, where she lived until her death in 1984.

When I returned to the aged care facility in Newtown, I sought out the old gentleman who had piqued my curiosity. He looked at me quizzically as I approached him.

'I know now about Marjorie Coleman and the flypaper poisonings,' I told him. 'Did you know her?'

He nodded his head and smiled broadly. 'Yes. Very, very well,' he replied.

'Did she do it?' I asked.

The old man pondered for a few moments and then, with a cheeky grin said, 'What do you think?'

CHAPTER NINE
THE LOVE OF A GUN

Section 18 of the *New South Wales Crimes Act 1900* (Cwlth) defines murder. The proofs that are required to commit the accused are that the thing done by the accused or omitted to be done was done maliciously and with reckless indifference to human life. The death occurred within a year and a day of that act. That definition has not changed over the years, nor has the serious consequences of that crime. Only the offender creates the individual, macabre profile of each homicide.

One in a while, a serial killer emerges. Traits that are usually attributed to such a person include insanity, thrill killing and hatred. But all serial killers I have met possess one distinguishing mark, that of selfishness.

Berwyn Rees was such a person. Born in 1949, he resided with his aged parents at the Ponderosa Caravan Park in Tomago, a suburb of Newcastle. Rees was an obese man, 188 centimetres tall and weighing 155 kilograms. The weight consisted of fat.

Rees was a loner, friendless both socially and romantically. His one desire in life was to possess and carry a gun. He joined the Belmont Pistol Club, but the rules and regulations of the sporting gun club did not suit his purposes and his membership lapsed. So did his authorisation to carry a firearm. But did it? Rees wasn't to be told when he could or could not have a gun.

His father owned an old yellow Valiant, not the best but good enough to get from one place to another. Rees wanted a gun collection and, without money, the only way he could get one would be by theft. In July 1977, he drove the Valiant to Sydney looking for a suitable gun shop to rob. The city was too busy with people so he continued on to the eastern suburbs, slowly cruising the streets until he reached Bronte Road in Bondi Junction. There he saw Nivison's Gun Shop. The place was ideal. He returned to his caravan home in Newcastle and developed his plan.

On 4 August, Rees hired a rental car in Newcastle and drove to the Bondi Junction gun shop. At 10am, he parked the hire car outside the shop, masked his face with a balaclava and armed himself with a .22 calibre sawn-off rifle he had prepared for the robbery.

Rees entered the shop. The only person inside was the manager, Raymond James. James was 26 years old, married, with one child. He turned to welcome his customer, only to find himself facing the wrong end of the sawn-off rifle.

Some years later Berwyn Rees would relate to police what then took place:

> *I entered the shop and produced a .22 calibre gun from my pocket. I told the man behind the counter to raise his hands. He*

made a lunge towards the other counter. I moved quickly and said something like, 'Don't be stupid. Lie down on your face.'

I went around the counter to see what he had been after.

I found a revolver that I later found to be fully loaded. As I moved back around the counter, another man entered the shop. He said something like, 'What's happening here?'

Christopher James Greenfield, a butcher from Northbridge in Sydney's north was a friend of Raymond James. He had come to the shop to say g'day to his mate. Instead, he had walked into an armed hold-up.

I waved the gun at him and told him to lie on his face. The proprietor of the shop, that was the man I made to lie down first, was saying something over and over again. I was afraid someone else would come in. I had some tape and I was going to tie the first guy up, but I only had enough tape for one guy. Both of them were lying down on the floor, so I shot the proprietor in the head. I stood over him and put the gun near the back of his head and pulled the trigger.

The other man started to say something and I shot him. I had to kill him so that he wouldn't recognise me again. I shot him in the back of the head also.

Rees removed his mask and closed and locked the front door of the gun shop. He then searched the manager's body for the keys to the safe. While he was at it, he stole a small amount of money from the victim's pocket.

Rees unlocked the safe and peered inside. It was as though he had found Aladdin's cave. Hand guns were everywhere. He took as many as he could carry away in two boxes he found in the shop: 18 hand guns, thousands of rounds of ammunition, together with gun holsters.

He took the stolen property to his car and then returned to the shop. Back inside, he arranged the two bodies in such a manner on the floor that they could not be readily seen through the front glass door. He then closed and locked the door behind him as he calmly left the scene.

Rees then drove to Mount Sugarloaf, about 20 kilometres from his Tomago home, threw the keys to the gun shop into a dam and hid his cache of weapons and ammunition under rocks. He returned the hire car in Newcastle and caught a bus back to his home, where he sat down to enjoy a hearty evening meal with his parents.

About the same time, a customer intending to make a purchase at Nivison's Gun Shop saw the two bodies through the shop window and contacted the police. Homicide detectives from Sydney's Criminal Investigation Branch began their investigation. The crime scene was photographed and fingerprinted and an itinerary of the stolen weapons with their serial numbers was circulated for the information of all police:

Stolen from the scene of a murder at Nivisons Pty Ltd, licensed pistol dealers, 121 Bronte Road, Bondi Junction on 4.8.77.

- *.357 Magnum Dan Wesson 6-chamber revolver*
- *.22 Walther self-loading pistol*
- *.357 Magnum Smith and Wesson 6-chamber revolver*
- *9mm Browning self-loading pistol*
- *.357 Magnum, Astra six-chamber revolver*
- *.38 Smith and Wesson six-chamber revolver*

- *.22 Bernadelli self-loading pistol*
- *.22 Higee Hi standard self-loading pistol*
- *.357 Magnum Astra six-chamber revolver*
- *.357 Magnum Astra six-chamber revolver*
- *.357 Magnum Astra six-chamber revolver*
- *.32 Browning self-loading pistol*
- *.357 Magnum Ruger six-chamber revolver*
- *.22 Ruger self-loading pistol*
- *.38 Smith and Wesson revolver*
- *.32 Browning self-loading pistol*
- *9mm Beretta self-loading pistol*
- *.357 Magnum Astra six-chamber revolver.*

Post-mortem examinations of both bodies were conducted and the calibre of the murder weapon was established. Despite wide media coverage, no useful information emerged that would assist the investigators. The amount of weaponry stolen indicated that more than one person was responsible. The inquiry had reached a stalemate.

Rees, in the meantime, retrieved his cache of stolen weapons from bushland and stored them out of sight in the annexe attached to his caravan. Three years passed before another fateful event would expose this offender.

A POLICEMAN'S EXECUTION

Mt Sugarloaf is a quiet picnic area located approximately 20 kilometres west of Newcastle in the Hunter Valley. The State Forestry Commission shares the mountain with the public, taking care of the Wattaga Forest.

About 11am on 24 November 1980, Cliff Hogbin, a 21-year-old Forestry Commission employee, was directed to investigate the sound of gunshots coming from the forest. The local police had been notified and would meet Hogbin at the picnic site.

Sergeant Keith Haydon was stationed at West Wallsend Lock-up as the Officer in Charge. Haydon was 36 years old, married, with three young children. He drove to Mt Sugarloaf to investigate the complaint.

He arrived there before the Forestry Commission worker to discover a yellow Valiant sedan parked just off the dirt road. Standing beside the vehicle was a very large, fat man. Sergeant Haydon parked the police car across the lone access track and approached the man. The officer began talking to the man and soon established that he was responsible for discharging a firearm.

The sergeant asked the man if he held a shooter's licence, which he said he did. He handed the licence to the police officer who saw that it was in the name of Berwyn Rees, born 25 April 1949. When Sergeant Haydon asked what weapon he had been using, Rees said, 'This one'.

He removed a .38 calibre Smith and Wesson revolver from his trousers pocket and without warning, fired three bullets into the sergeant's body. The officer fell to the ground and Rees got in the Valiant. However, he couldn't get past the police car which was blocking the access road. The keys to the vehicle were in Haydon's pocket.

Rees walked back to where the police officer lay rolling on the ground attempting to get to his feet. The offender placed his gun at the back of the sergeant's head and, with one further shot, killed him.

Rees searched the dead police officer and located the keys to his car. He took Haydon's service revolver from its holster and gathered the policeman's notebook from where he had dropped it after he was shot. Rees moved the police car off the road and left the scene in the yellow Valiant.

The Forestry Commission worker, Cliff Hogbin, was almost at the scene of the shooting. As he drew nearer, he was approached from the opposite direction by the offender. Both cars stopped on the narrow road and Hogbin leant from his vehicle and asked Rees whether he had heard any shooting in the area. Rees replied in the negative and both men continued on their journeys, Hogbin towards the murder scene and Rees to freedom.

The young forestry officer had noted and written down the registration number of the car in which Rees was travelling. The gunman had seen Hogbin do this and later told police that he stopped his car, with the intention of returning and killing Hogbin but decided against this tactic. That decision would prove to be a big mistake.

Hogbin reached the scene of the police officer's murder and was shocked at what he saw. The young man had plenty of common sense and initiative. After confirming that Sergeant Haydon was dead, he went to the police car and, after working out how to use the radio handset, called into the mouthpiece stating his location and that a police office had been shot. He gave the police radio operator a description of Berwyn Rees, together with the type of vehicle he was driving and its registration number.

The information was circulated immediately over the police radio network and coded as a Signal One (officer in trouble). Years earlier, a signals code book had been introduced into police use, giving a series of numbers for various crimes and incidents. The book was meant to thwart the ever-intrusive media over what was happening, but when the reporters obtained a copy of the book, the codes were taken out of operations. Signal One, however, had been retained. It meant 'officer in trouble' and always brought an immediate response from other police.

Rees had driven about 40 kilometres to the small township of Beresfield when he was seen by a patrolling police officer, Constable Alexander Pietruska. The officer notified the police radio that he was following the suspect and asked for assistance.

Rees became stationary in traffic behind a coal truck and the police constable decided to act. He left his police car, ran to where Rees had stopped and ordered him from his car. Rees obliged.

'Where's your gun?' demanded the police officer, who had his own revolver pointed at Rees.

'On the back seat,' replied Rees.

Pietruska began to look for the gun and was satisfied when he located it in a bag on the back seat. He assumed that he had found the murder weapon.

During his search the constable had momentarily taken his eyes away from Rees and failed to realise that the offender was multi-armed. He turned to face Rees who had now produced another hand gun from his pocket. Again without warning, Rees shot the police officer twice through his stomach.

Pietruska fell to the ground and crawled behind a stationary car. He rolled across the road as Rees appeared, gun in hand and firing, intent on killing him. When the gun was out of ammunition, Rees reached into his pocket for more bullets and began to reload. Other police officers who had responded to Pietruska's call for assistance arrived in time to subdue Rees before he killed the wounded officer.

Pietruska was conveyed to Maitland Hospital, where he would recover from his near fatal encounter with Berwyn Rees. The offender was driven with detectives to Maitland Police Station to be interviewed. He showed no remorse over the murder of Sergeant Haydon. In fact, his attitude was the exact opposite. He was hungry and ordered a hot meal and coffee, which he eagerly consumed.

Rees was taken back to the site where he had slain the police sergeant. No longer was the Mt Sugarloaf picnic area peaceful and quiet. Fresh blood marked the spot where Keith Haydon had been executed.

A 'run around' was conducted, with Rees re-enacting his role in the shooting. Venturing slightly into bushland to the side of the recreational area, police saw trees stripped of bark, the result of bullet impact. Rocks also showed the scars of gunfire. This was Berwyn Rees' playground, which he frequented regularly, acting out childhood games with real guns and ammunition. Armed with the weapons he had stolen from the Bondi Junction gun shop three years earlier, he would play Cowboys and Indians, with him as the hero and the trees and rocks as the bad guys.

Rees led police to where he had buried Sergeant Haydon's service revolver and notebook, then back to his caravan annexe, where a large cache of guns was discovered. His aged parents stood by watching, shattered as they were told of their son's crimes.

The discovery of Rees' weapons prompted police to ask the obvious question, 'Where did they come from?'

Rees' answer was spontaneous. 'I got them from a gun shop at Bondi Junction. I decided to hold it up and get about five revolvers. I went down and did it and I had to shoot them. The manager, he made a dive for something. I found he was going for a loaded .357 Magnum. I killed them both and that's where the pistols are from.'

When asked what he did with the murder weapon, the offender replied, 'I threw it off the Toule Street bridge. I got rid of the shop keys in a dam near Mt Sugarloaf.'

JUDGMENT DAY

On 20 January 1981, Berwyn Rees appeared in the Newcastle Court of Petty Sessions charged with three counts of murder and one of attempted murder. In an unprecedented move, the Magistrate ordered that Rees be handcuffed because of the threatening ambience of the big man. He was committed to stand trial on each charge.

Three months later, in April 1981, Rees was found guilty of all charges in Sydney's Central Criminal Court. He was sentenced to penal servitude for life.

A detective classified Rees as a serial killer and asked him what it felt like to kill more than one person.

'The first one is strange, but then it's easy,' was Rees' reply.

CHAPTER TEN
LOOSE LIPS

Sergeant Jack Errington was a uniformed officer stationed at Rockdale, a southern suburb of Sydney. He was also a classmate of mine, joining the force in 1951, just weeks before his thirtieth birthday. That was the age limit placed on applicants for the police force in those days and Jack, understandably, soon acquired the nickname of 'Pappy'.

At 10pm on 20 April 1968, Jack received a telephone call at Rockdale Station, allegedly from the licensee of the Bexley Hotel, advising that he was having trouble with hoodlums. Pappy drove the police car (PD) to the hotel and parked nearby in Kingsland Road, Bexley. He was in the hotel for only a few minutes. The complaint was bogus.

On returning to where he had left the PD, he discovered just why he had been sent on such a wild goose chase. The car had been stolen.

A search of the area was made by a number of police officers and the car was soon located, dumped about a kilometre from the hotel. Wires hanging from the dashboard revealed what the thieves were seeking. The police radio transmitter and receiver were missing.

This disturbing news was an omen of things to come. What started out as a simple, routine police inquiry would set off a chain of events that could easily have caused the deaths of a number of innocent people, including police.

FRIEND OR FOE?

Forty-six-year-old John Robert Dorling was a well-known businessman who operated a car repair facility in Kogarah, in Sydney's south. He was married and lived with his wife in Earlwood, and regarded as a thoroughly respectable member of the community.

Through his business transactions of attending motor accidents and repairing damaged vehicles, he became associated with a number of local police officers. Some of these relationships developed into friendships. Dorling owned a speedboat and was an avid waterskier. He fostered his friendships with the police by inviting them to go waterskiing with him on their days off duty.

What was regarded as casual 'work chatter' took place on these outings, with police innocently divulging matters of little interest or concern to Dorling. Remarks such as, 'Night shift's a bore because we have to do the mail run to Newtown at midnight and we're out of our patrol for incoming jobs for up to two hours', or, 'We're short-staffed and there's only two cars to cover the division this week', or, 'There's no car on tonight as we have to do a hospital guard'. Innocent chatter? Perhaps. But during World War II there was a popular saying: 'Loose lips sink ships'.

THE CRIME COMMENCES

Between April 1968—after the police radio had been stolen—and April 1969, a pattern of crime developed in Sydney where the secretary managers of licensed registered clubs were being kidnapped from their homes by three armed and masked offenders. In each case, the managers had returned to their homes after closing hours, leaving their respective club locked up for the night. The robbers would appear at the managers' homes and take their quarry back to the club, where they were forced to open the safe. The victims would then be bound and gagged and left at the club.

The majority of the abductions were from homes in the St George district, although the targeted clubs were scattered in their locations. Detectives from the Criminal Investigation Branch (CIB) soon became involved and, after conferring with local area detectives, a plan of action was formulated on the known facts:

1. A police radio was used to monitor police activity in the proposed crime location. (Victims had reported hearing police broadcasts over a radio carried by the offenders.)
2. Most of the crimes occurred during a public holiday weekend, when larger than usual amounts of money were being held by the clubs.

3. The thieves began their operations in the police patrols of Kogarah, Rockdale and Hurstville (in No. 12 Division).
4. The offenders appeared to have knowledge of the radio call signs used by police in this division.

The plan was put into operation on 27 April 1969, the Easter weekend. Detectives from the CIB and No. 12 Division formed the crews of additional police cars to patrol the St George district. The cars were allocated car call signs that would be unfamiliar to any illegitimate listener—in fact, to anyone not associated with the police operation. Crews were requested to maintain police radio silence wherever possible in order to frustrate the offenders. The rule was only to be broken in the event of extreme urgency.

At 11.30 that evening, six detectives—the crews of two of the special patrol vehicles—met at Hurstville Police Station to discuss areas to be covered and other strategies. I was a member on one car crew, at that time holding the rank of detective sergeant.

ACTION TIME

Malcolm Underwood was the secretary manager of the East Hills Golf Club situated in southwest Sydney. At 6pm on 27 April 1969, Easter Sunday, he closed and locked the club early and drove to his daughter's home at Mortdale before continuing on to his own home in Bristol Road, Hurstville. The time was then 11.15pm.

Loose Lips

Underwood had been home for only 15 minutes when the front doorbell rang. When he opened the door, he was confronted by three armed men, with stockings pulled down over their faces and wearing Beatle-style wigs. Underwood tried to close the door, but the men smashed the glass and forced their way inside. The club manager was pushed into a chair, but would later relate that the offenders were reasonably considerate of his wellbeing.

One of the men said, 'We don't want anything from you at all, we don't want to hurt you. All we want is the money from the club.'

They grabbed Underwood by the arms and were about to take him from his home, when one of the men looked out a front window and exclaimed, 'There's a car outside. Watch out, it's the cops.'

Many would call the arrival of the police 'good fortune', others might say 'good police work'. Both are applicable.

A telephone call had been received at Hurstville Police Station ten minutes earlier. The caller reported to the station sergeant the breaking of glass and a possible domestic dispute at a house in Bristol Road. The local PD was at the station and the crew, Sergeant Keith Hart and Constable John Cribb, were sent to investigate. No radio contact had been made and so no one—neither other police nor the offenders—was aware the police were on their way.

Approximately ten minutes later, a further telephone call was received at Hurstville Station to the effect that the two police officers from the PD were in serious trouble. The six detectives from the special patrols were informed by the station sergeant, and they hurried to Bristol Road. Once again, no radio contact was made.

Sergeant Hart and Constable Cribb had been expecting a domestic disturbance but on their arrival at the house in Bristol Road, they noticed a gold 1967 Holden sedan, bearing the registration plates DJM442, parked outside.

A quick inspection of the vehicle by torchlight revealed a number of army-type haversacks lying on the rear floor and a wireless aerial clipped to the gutter of the car's roof. The motor was hot, with the keys hanging from the ignition. With what proved to be great foresight, the police removed those keys.

The two officers then entered the front yard of the house as four men exited through the front door. Three were masked and armed and appeared to be using the fourth man as a shield.

Constable Cribb drew his service revolver and confronted the men in the darkness, shining his torch on them. He shouted, 'Police here, stay where you are.'

One of the masked men replied, 'Back off, we've got him with us. If you don't back off, we'll shoot him. Drop your guns or I'll blow his guts out.'

The two officers backed off a little and switched off their torches as the men edged towards their car. When they discovered the ignition keys had been removed, the offenders panicked and fled on foot, releasing Malcolm Underwood in the process.

The three crooks ran into Croot Park, a reserve opposite Underwood's home. Cribb and Hart pursued them. Gunshots were fired at the officers, who returned the fire.

Bristol Road was not far from Hurstville Police Station and the special patrol detectives quickly arrived at the scene. They joined the PD crew and assisted in a search of the park, where it was considered the offenders might be hiding.

The gunmen, however, had run through the park and emerged on the other side, in Romani Avenue, where one of the gang parted company with his colleagues. The other two entered the home of Kevin Peters through an unlocked front door.

Kevin and his wife were in bed. They were awakened by one of the men when he held a sawn-off rifle close to their heads.

'I want the keys to your car out the front,' he screamed at the startled couple. 'The Valiant keys, the Valiant.'

Kevin took a bunch of keys from his bedhead and attempted to remove the car keys from the key ring. The gunman became more agitated and shouted, 'Give me the lot. Hurry up, the cops are chasing us.'

The two offenders ran from the house and had just entered Kevin Peter's car when police arrived and surrounded the vehicle. The passenger pointed a revolver at a detective who approached the car. The officer was armed and when he threatened to shoot, the offender dropped his weapon.

A young detective moved to the driver's side of the Valiant and, as he did so, the man sprang from the car, aimed a pistol at the officer's head and yelled, 'Get away, get away! I'll shoot you.'

The officer who had control of the passenger called on the driver to drop his gun. Instead, the offender turned and aimed the weapon at the detective. The policeman fired first, the bullet hitting the offender in the side of his body. He dropped to the roadway and was quickly subdued and handcuffed.

The passenger then attempted to talk his way out of his dilemma. He pulled the wig from his head and said, 'Can I see you for a moment? Can I make a deal?'

'What sort of a deal?' the detective asked.

'Let me go and I'll fix you up later,' was the plea.

'You've got to be joking,' the police officer replied.

'Don't you recognise me? I'm John Dorling from Dorling Brothers. Christ, what a mess. But it had to happen. Did the copper get hit?' he asked.

Dorling had met the detective on one of his waterskiing excursions and hoped that the association might have helped him. He was wrong.

He was searched and, apart from the .45 calibre Colt pistol he had dropped, he was fitted with a shoulder holster and a second fully loaded pistol was found in his trousers pocket.

The wounded man, when shot by police, had dropped a 9mm Browning automatic pistol, fully loaded with 13 rounds of ammunition. In his coat pocket, he carried a fully loaded .32 calibre Colt pistol and a spare magazine of eight bullets. The offenders certainly meant business.

Before being conveyed to St George Hospital, the wounded man was identified as Leslie Gordon Lockman, born 28 July 1930. He was admitted to hospital and placed under police guard. His condition was not life threatening.

The third offender had eluded the police search, but his identity was soon confirmed as Trevor John Sawyer, born on 29 July 1941. Sawyer was a convicted criminal and his latest address at Marrickville was watched by police. He never returned.

An inspection of the offenders' vehicle revealed that it had been fitted with illegally manufactured numberplates.

The car had been reported stolen from Cabramatta two months earlier.

A fully loaded .38 calibre Webley revolver was retrieved from the glove box. The stolen police radio receiver, taken 12 months earlier from the Rockdale PD, was located in the cabin. A number of haversacks, intended to be used for carrying away money from the targeted clubs, was also found in the car.

PUTTING THE JIGSAW TOGETHER

Following the arrests, police began the task of identifying the origins of the weapons recovered and establishing just what prior offences had been committed by the trio. The weapons included:

- .45 Colt pistol
- .38 Webley revolver
- .32 Colt pistol
- 9mm Browning pistol
- .32 Walther pistol
- .30 US M1 sawn-off carbine rifle
- .32 Browning pistol
- a number of loaded, spare magazines to fit the above weapons.

Sundry items included shoulder holsters, wigs, masks, walkie-talkies, a stolen police radio, side cutters, gloves, rope, tape and the haversacks.

John Dorling's home at Earlwood was visited and his wife spoken to. An interesting conversation took place when detectives informed Mrs Dorling of her husband's arrest during an armed abduction.

'I knew John was involved in hold-ups. You remember that one at Canterbury RSL where one man had a police uniform? I should have done more. He had a police uniform, a sergeant's uniform, in his wardrobe for days before that and it disappeared afterwards,' she said.

The armed robbery at the Canterbury–Hurlstone Park RSL Club took place on the night of 8 December 1968. The .38 calibre Webley revolver recovered in the offenders' possession was stolen from a security guard during the commission of that offence. Three armed men, one dressed as a police officer, were responsible. The staff were locked in a strongroom by the offenders after the club had closed. I remembered the robbery well because I had been on night duty and attended the scene of the crime.

Several nights prior to their arrest, the two offenders and Trevor Sawyer committed an armed robbery on the staff at the Skyline drive-in at Bass Hill in Sydney's southwest. Other robberies and stolen motor vehicles they had used during their 12-month crime spree were identified. With the arrest of the offenders, the kidnappings and club raids ceased.

On 2 May 1969, five days after the Hurstville shoot-out between police and the offenders, Mrs Laura Brown of Crosby Avenue, Hurstville, a street adjoining Romani Avenue, was disturbed by a man as he crawled from beneath her house. He looked dishevelled and weak. The man left before the police arrived.

A search was made under the floor area of the home and police discovered a bottle of water and a fully loaded

Browning automatic pistol. Both items were examined for fingerprints and those of Trevor John Sawyer were identified on each article. He had concealed himself under the house for five days after the arrest of his co-offenders before attempting to fully escape from the area.

THE CHARGES

Leslie Lockman recovered from his gunshot wound and, when released from hospital was charged similarly to the charges that had already been preferred against John Dorling. Those matters included assault and robbery whilst armed; kidnapping, breaking, entering and stealing; shoot with intent to avoid apprehension; abduction; larceny of motor vehicles; firearm offences; and breach of the Wireless and Telegraph Act.

On 17 July 1970, John Robert Dorling appeared before His Honour Judge Harvey Prior at the Sydney Quarter Sessions where he pleaded guilty to four of those matters. He was sentenced to 10 years' hard labour for burglary being armed; five years for kidnapping; six years for being armed, break, enter and rob; and two years for larceny of a motor vehicle.

All up, he was sentenced to 15 years' hard labour with an aggregate non-parole period of six years. This sentence was subsequently appealed, resulting in all sentences being served concurrently and a non-parole date fixed as not before 31 December 1974.

On 21 August 1970, Leslie Gordon Lockman appeared at the same court, where he pleaded guilty to four charges.

His sentences were nine years and four months for burglary being armed; nine years for kidnapping; six years for being armed, commit break, enter and rob; and two years for larceny of a motor vehicle. This amounted to a total sentence of nine years and four months, with a non-parole period of four years and six months.

The convictions and sentences against each accused were considered by the Crown to be sufficient punishment. No evidence was offered in respect to other outstanding charges and they were dismissed.

THE SUCCESS OF THE PLANNING

Trevor John Sawyer was 28 years old at the time of these offences. Although a continuing criminal offender with 15 prior convictions against his name, Sawyer managed to avoid police detection after his escape. To date, he has never been located.

Sawyer had known John Dorling for a number of years, the two having met initially through being involved in the motor industry. Leslie Lockman had been introduced into the group by Sawyer and was the car driver on the trio's criminal escapades.

John Robert Dorling was released from jail on parole on 31 December 1974. He returned to the family car repair business at Kogarah and has since led an apparent crime-free life.

Leslie Gordon Lockman was released from Silverwater Jail on 23 December 1979. He resettled at Sadlier in Sydney's southwest, remaining free of trouble until 1992, when he was charged and convicted of cultivating and supplying a prohibited drug. He was sentenced to four months in jail.

It is impossible to minimise to any degree the seriousness of the behaviour of Dorling, Lockman or Sawyer. Each man was multi-armed with fully loaded weapons and carried spare magazines for each gun. Their willingness to use those weapons was apparent when they fired shots at pursuing police officers.

CHAPTER ELEVEN

THERE'S ALWAYS A CLUE

At 9.15am on Wednesday 3 January 1968, Sidney Frederick Foy answered frantic knocking on the door of his home unit at 16/189 President Avenue, Kogarah, in Sydney's south. Standing outside were two petrified young girls. They told him that something terrible had happened to one of their mothers.

Mr Foy left the children in the care of his wife and cautiously climbed the stairs to unit 17 on the floor above his own. He had no idea of what he might find.

The timber door of the unit had been forced open and the broken lock hung from one side. Mr Foy gently pushed the door open and looked inside. Lying on his back, unconscious and critically wounded from a bullet wound to the right side of his head, lay 41-year-old John James Warren, known to Foy as a regular visitor to that unit. Alongside him was a revolver.

Mr Foy heard a faint cry for help coming from the back of the unit and saw the legs of a female protruding from a doorway into the hall. He went to the woman's aid. She was 50-year-old Molly Campbell, and she had a bullet wound behind her right ear that was bleeding profusely. Molly was covered in blood.

'Look what's happened to me. I can't hear! I can't hear!' she wailed.

Mr Foy moved to the main bedroom and caught his breath when he saw the bodies of a man and woman on a double bed. Dressed in a red shortie nightdress and lying on her back was Glory Lorraine McGlinn. The 32-year-old woman had suffered a bullet wound to the right side of her nose. Gunpowder surrounded the wound, indicating the gun had been discharged against her face. Beside her was the naked body of a 22-year-old male who had two bullet holes in the left side of his face. Both the woman and the man were obviously dead.

Mr Foy ran back downstairs to his own unit and telephoned Kogarah Police Station to report what he had found. He then rang the Ambulance Service.

The unit at 189 President Avenue was isolated and placed under police guard, awaiting the arrival of the police scientific crime scene personnel and the city coroner. The injured John Warren and Molly Campbell were conveyed to St George Hospital, where both were admitted. Warren was classified as critical and Campbell as serious.

Mrs Campbell remained conscious, the bullet in her head having passed around the back of her skull without penetrating her brain cavity. I was allowed to interview her at the hospital before she underwent surgery.

'My ears are ringing. I'm so hot. He broke in the door like a madman and shot Glory and Brian. Then he shot me,' she told me.

When I asked her who had broken into the unit, Mrs Campbell replied, 'Johnny. Johnny Warren. I knew he'd do it! He was insanely jealous and thought she would put him in, put him in for that shooting. Are they dead?'

That was all the conversation I had with Mrs Campbell before medical staff moved in to provide further treatment. I was puzzled by her short reference to Glory McGlinn 'putting Warren in for that shooting'. What shooting was she referring to?

Mrs Campbell would not be interviewed again. Her condition suddenly deteriorated and she lapsed into a coma. She died the following day without regaining consciousness.

Police investigations naturally centred on the crime scene at Kogarah. The three-bedroom unit was one of 18 in a modern, redbrick structure near the western shore of Botany Bay. The furnishing was expensive. Children's dolls and other Christmas gifts covered the plush carpet in the lounge room. An ornamental Christmas tree and dozens of Christmas cards added to the decorations. A well-stocked bar occupied one corner of the lounge room, with two large wall mirrors reflecting the opulence of the residence.

A pool of congealing blood and the .38 calibre Smith and Wesson revolver on the floor were incongruous in the surroundings. Sitting on a chair, peering at the spot where John Warren had apparently shot himself, sat a stuffed toy clown with a large smiling face.

THE VICTIMS

What events led to the shootings of 3 January 1968 is best explained by an outline of each victim's background and the weapon involved.

The 22-year-old deceased male was Brian Bowman, born in Queensland on 30 January 1945. He was a married man, living apart from his wife in George Street, Dover Heights, in the eastern suburbs of Sydney. Bowman held a permanent job as a salesman in a store at Bondi Junction. He also worked during the evenings as a casual steward at the Eastern Suburbs Leagues Club. That was where he met Glory McGlinn. On 2 January 1968, Bowman escorted McGlinn to her Kogarah home unit for what became a fatal one-night stand.

Glory Lorraine Campbell was born in Sydney on 28 October 1936 and married Hugh Gordon McGlinn in 1956. The couple lived in Kingston Road, Camperdown, and in 1961 their daughter Kim was born. The marriage was troubled and turbulent, with Glory often leaving the home to live with a former boyfriend named John Warren.

John Warren was not Glory's only boyfriend and she earned the reputation of being liberal with her sexual favours. During 1967, Hugh McGlinn served divorce papers on his wife who was, by then, residing at the Kogarah address. The unit had been purchased by Warren for occupancy by Glory, her daughter Kim and her mother Molly Campbell.

Little need be related of Molly Campbell, other than she was the mother of Glory McGlinn and was born in Sydney on 25 March 1918. At the time of her death, she was residing at the Kogarah unit. Glory confided in her mother, who was aware of her relationships and activities. Molly condoned her daughter's behaviour.

John James Warren was an enigma. Born in Sydney on 14 July 1926, he was a caring husband to his wife and four children. However, away from home he assumed another persona. He worked as an illegal SP bookmaker, associated with heavy criminals and gained the reputation of a standover man and 'gun for hire'.

He married his wife Betty in November 1950 and resided with her and their children at Bonar Street, in Arncliffe, south of Sydney. Mrs Warren was aware of her husband's association with Glory McGlinn but preferred to let the relationship dwindle naturally rather than throw her own marriage and family into disorder. When the relationship broke down in December 1967, John Warren became emotionally disturbed. He began to brood when his efforts of reconciliation with Glory McGlinn were rejected.

The firearm used in the Kogarah slayings was a .38 calibre Smith and Wesson special, six-shot revolver. Five bullets had been discharged, with one bullet remaining in the chamber when the weapon was recovered. The revolver had been purchased in July 1967 from Sydney gunsmith Jack Hochstadt by a licensed pistol holder, Ronald Joseph Lee. The new owner had the firearm for only two weeks before it was stolen from his car while parked in Redfern. The theft was reported to police. John Warren's wife Betty was employed by Ronald Lee. Police drew their own conclusions about how John Warren was able to identify Lee's car and knew that it contained a firearm.

THE KILLINGS

At 9am on 3 January 1968, John Warren kissed his wife goodbye and left his Arncliffe home in the family car, a 1964 Morris 1100 sedan. He drove to Banks Street, Kogarah, and after parking, walked the short distance to the block of units in President Avenue. Tucked inside his belt was the fully loaded Smith and Wesson revolver, disguised by the lightweight jacket he was wearing.

John Warren climbed the staircase until he was standing outside the door of unit 17. He was a powerfully built man and it took little effort for him to break open the door and enter the dwelling.

Six-year-old Kim McGlinn was playing with a girlfriend in the lounge room when the door burst open. Warren, in an uncontrollable rage, drew the revolver from his waist and stormed into the main bedroom. Glory McGlinn jumped up from the bed, but was held by Warren who placed the gun against her face and fired. She dropped back to the bed and died. The enraged Warren walked to the opposite side of the bed and shot the awakening Brian Bowman twice through the head.

Molly Campbell, wakened by the disturbance, had reached the doorway of her bedroom, when she encountered Warren. He pointed the revolver at her and shot her in the back of the head as she retreated.

Warren returned to the lounge room and, in the presence of the two little girls, lifted the gun to his head and shot himself. He remained unconscious in St George Hospital until his death at 2.50am on 22 January 1968, almost three weeks later.

Police searched the premises but uncovered nothing that might explain the motive for the murders other than extreme jealousy. Bundles of banknotes wrapped in brown paper and totalling over $2000 were located in the bottom of a wardrobe in Molly Campbell's room.

Mrs Campbell's last words were still troubling the investigators: 'He was insanely jealous and thought she would put him in, put him in for that shooting.' Information coming from the lips of a dying woman must surely be a clue. Police decided to backtrack and review reports of shootings, solved or unsolved, fatal or otherwise, in which John James Warren was a common denominator.

THE CLUE CONNECTS

Coincidentally, on the same day as the murders, 3 January 1968, a reward poster was published and signed by NSW Premier Robert Askin. Headed 'Suspected Murder', the poster read:

At about 7.30pm on Sunday, the 25th June, 1967, Richard Gabriel Reilly, aged 58 years, was shot and killed in Manning Road, Double Bay. The post-mortem examination disclosed that death was due to a bullet wound in the neck. There were a number of other wounds found on the body which were caused by pellets discharged from a shotgun.

Notice is hereby given that a reward of five thousand dollars ($5,000) will be paid by the Government of New South Wales for such information as will lead to the arrest of the person or persons responsible for the death of Richard Gabriel Reilly. In addition, His Excellency the Governor will be *advised to extend a free pardon to any accomplice, not being the person who actually committed the crime, who first gives such information.*

When John Warren died, a sigh of relief was exhaled by a certain Sydney criminal known by the pseudonym 'Joseph Smith'. Three weeks later, on 25 January 1968, he telephoned Sydney CIB and spoke to the detective in charge of the shooting murder of Richard Reilly.

'I know who did it. All I want is the reward,' said the informant.

An immediate interview was requested by the police, but the caller backed off and hung up the telephone. The following day, however, 'Joseph Smith' rang again. This time he agreed to meet with police at Fairfield in Sydney's west. Two senior detectives were assigned for the interview and, after meeting with him and gaining his confidence, Smith agreed to tell them everything.

The informant led the two detectives to the Georges River at Picnic Point and indicated where the shotgun involved in Reilly's murder had been tossed. He was then taken to a secret location where a 40-page recorded interview was held with him over a period of nearly 18 hours. In the interview, Smith outlined his knowledge of not one but two murders.

BACKGROUND

Richard Reilly was born on 18 November 1909 and resided at 9 Cammeray Avenue, Castle Cove, in Sydney's northern suburbs. Reilly had a criminal record and was a minder for reputed abortionists Dr Stewart Jones and 'Dr' Ivan Marcovics. At the time of his murder, Reilly was engaged in the security of illegal gambling establishments, mainly baccarat that was played at the Kellet Club at Kings Cross.

At 7.30pm on Sunday 25 June 1967, Reilly left the home of a woman friend at 13 Manning Road, Double Bay, in Sydney's eastern suburbs. As he walked to his new blue Maserati coupe, he was approached by a female armed with a small calibre rifle and a male carrying a 10 gauge shotgun.

Reilly ran to his car as the couple began shooting at him. Although critically wounded, he was able to drive into Old South Head Road before collapsing at the steering wheel. The Maserati rolled backwards onto the footpath and into the plate glass window of a gift shop. Reilly was dead.

A search of his body revealed that he did indeed 'live the life of Reilly'. The sum of $1983 was contained in his wallet, a princely sum in 1967. Also in his possession were four personal diaries in which the names of 389 individuals were listed, some of very dubious character.

Reilly was well connected and investigators began checking these names in an effort to locate a suspect for his murder. They had met with no success, until the appearance of the informer Joseph Smith.

'Who shot Reilly?' was the main question the detectives put to Smith.

'Johnny Warren,' he replied. 'He's dead now, so he can't get me.'

John James Warren's name had also appeared in one of Reilly's diaries and he had been interviewed as a suspect early in the police inquiry, particularly as he was known to have an intense hatred for the dead man. The feud had arisen when Warren wanted to organise his own gambling syndicate in Kings Cross, but was muscled out by Reilly. Warren, however, had an airtight alibi. He was with a woman friend at the time of Reilly's murder and kilometres away from the crime scene.

Who was this woman friend? Glory Lorraine McGlinn.

The information supplied by Joseph Smith, while exciting, needed corroboration. Detectives in charge of the shootings of Glory McGlinn, Brian Bowman, Molly Campbell and John Warren were contacted by Smith's case officers to see whether any evidence existed that might implicate Warren in Richard Reilly's murder.

Meanwhile, police divers were searching the Georges River at Picnic Point in an effort to locate the firearm Smith claimed to have been used in Reilly's murder. After eight days of searching, they recovered a .22 Gevarm rifle and the barrel of a Parker Hale safari rifle. The Gevarm weapon proved identical to that used in the murder of Clive Henry Eldridge, aged 50, on 22 April 1967. Eldridge was shot five times at Neutral Bay in Sydney's north.

THE PLOT

Charles Edward Rennerson was a 70-year-old money lender who lived in Ocean Street, Woollahra. He was associated with an SP bookmaker named James Cyril Walker, aged 60. Walker resided in Blues Point Road, North Sydney, and gave as his official source of employment the more acceptable occupation of surveyor's assistant. Richard Reilly had borrowed a substantial amount of money from Rennerson and refused to repay the debt. This infuriated the money lender to such a degree that he asked his friend Walker to locate a person prepared to murder Reilly. A contract price of $8000 was mentioned.

Clive Eldridge worked at a Kings Cross garage as a car washer and was known to be a police informant. He was probably aware of the murder contract on Reilly and therefore became a threat to Rennerson. Eldridge's life also became the subject of a negotiable contract, this one for $6000.

The informant Joseph Smith was approached to fulfil both contracts and readily agreed. But he was not prepared to do the slayings himself. He obtained the services of his friend John Warren who would have been prepared to murder Reilly without payment, such was his hatred for the man. Smith told Warren and Glory McGlinn that a wealthy man wanted Reilly dead.

Warren already had in his possession the firearms required for the hits on both Reilly and Eldridge—the Gevarm rifle and the Parker Hale safari rifle. Both weapons had been purchased by Warren from a Sydney gunsmith who later identified Warren from a photograph.

On 22 April 1967, Smith accompanied Warren to Kurraba Road, Neutral Bay, and watched Warren shoot Eldridge as he left the apartment of a girlfriend.

Warren was in the mood for killing. He had his personal collection of people he wanted dead. This included three heavy criminals: Lenny McPherson, Stanley Smith and Steward John Regan. They were his opposition. NSW Police officer Detective Sergeant David James had also been marked down for execution. David James was responsible for closing down Warren's SP business at Liverpool. Warren's next target, however, would be Richard Gabriel Reilly, and plans were made to carry out that murder.

Warren rented a garage in the inner Sydney suburb of Enmore in which he kept a stolen car, the safari rifle and a 10 gauge shotgun. He covertly watched his victim for two months before deciding the best location for the job would be when Reilly was leaving the home of a woman friend at Double Bay. Warren knew he would only get the one chance to eliminate the man he detested and so, to ensure his proficiency was first class in the use of firearms, he travelled to bushland in Sydney's southwest for target practice. On 25 June 1967, he gunned down and killed Reilly while the informant Joseph Smith and Glory McGlinn stood by as interested onlookers.

Apart from indicating to police the location of the firearms used in both murders, Smith also took them to bushland where he had accompanied Warren during his shooting practice. Spent cartridges were recovered from the sites and later Forensic Ballistics examinations proved they were from Reilly's murder weapon.

The chance of earning the $5000 reward urged Smith on. He told police he would be prepared to give evidence at any future court proceedings that might take place.

THE ARRESTS

On 15 March 1968, James Cyril Walker was arrested by investigating police officers. He admitted making offers of up to $8000 and $12,000 for the murders of Clive Henry Eldridge and Richard Gabriel Reilly respectively. He claimed, however, that the contracts were not accepted. Walker stated that he believed John Warren was responsible for both murders as he did 'dirty work' for the money lender Charles Edward Rennerson.

Rennerson was arrested on 16 March 1968 and admitted to police that he knew both the deceased men, plus John Warren. That was the total of his admissions.

Both men were charged with accessory before the fact of murder and of conspiracy with John Warren to commit murder. On 18 March 1968, they appeared in the Paddington Court of Petty Sessions and were remanded to appear at the Coroner's Court. Bail was refused by Magistrate Murray Farquhar.

The coroner's hearing took place on 8 and 9 April 1968 before Mr Loomes, SM. Evidence given during the two-day hearing included the last words uttered by Molly Campbell on 3 January 1968 at St George Hospital. Both Rennerson and Walker were committed to stand trial at the Central Criminal Court on all charges.

Application was made by the defence lawyers to the NSW Attorney General stating that the prosecution case was weak, and that no reasonable jury would convict on the evidence. In June of the same year, a decision was made not to proceed with the charges and the two suspects were discharged and released from custody.

What promised to be a financial bonanza for informant Joseph Smith fell flat. He received a $250 gratuity for his information. This amount may have proved to be well balanced when consideration was given to a greater benefit he received, that of immunity from prosecution for his active involvement in two murders.

Five people were murdered by John James Warren, a hardened criminal who could not overcome his insane jealousy. Some of the murders may have remained unsolved for years had it not been for a few words uttered by a dying woman in the presence of police.

There's always a clue. It just has to be recognised.

CHAPTER TWELVE
FATAL ODYSSEY

'He's a madman on the loose, possessed by the devil', were the words uttered by a Sydney radio station announcer on the afternoon of 31 January 1984. They were definitely not the words five hostages being held at gunpoint in a car wanted to hear to describe their captor. The gunman was already agitated and the announcer's portrayal of him only added to his anxiety and anger.

The NSW Police negotiators were not impressed by the broadcast either. All their efforts to resolve a siege situation now seemed to have been negated. They shook their heads in disbelief, stunned that broadcasters didn't realise crooks listened to the radio. In fact, listening to the radio is their modus operandi (MO), to ascertain the reaction and response to their crime. The police Media Relations Branch soon got to all the radio stations with the message: 'Stop dramatising'.

BACKGROUND

Hakki Bahadi Atahan was 35 years old and lived alone in Marshall Street, Manly. He was born in Turkey and migrated to Australia when he was twenty-one. Atahan was a married man with one small child. When he arrived in Sydney, he began working as a taxi driver. However, a heavy gambling habit, with its associated losses, caused his marriage to break-up and ultimately lead to divorce.

Atahan became friendly with a prostitute from the neighbouring northern beaches suburb of Queenscliff. He moved in as her minder and controlled most of her earnings as well as her protection. But even this extra income failed to satisfy his gambling losses, so he moved into the world of crime.

It wasn't long before he established a lengthy criminal history, gaining convictions for theft, malicious injury and, eventually, armed robbery. The latter became second nature to Atahan who, unsurprisingly, went unopposed by his victims when armed with a pistol and sawn-off rifle.

Between 11 March 1983 and 9 January 1984, Atahan committed 17 armed robberies, mostly on banks. In this 10-month period, his crimes netted him $175,820.

Like many crooks, money meant little to him. It was simply a commodity for gambling and living the high life. 'Easy come, easy go', was his style. He took holidays in his native Turkey, travelled to the United States, bought expensive jewellery and a Ford Landau. The money, however, was never enough. He always wanted more.

A BUSY SCHEDULE

At 3pm on 31 January 1984, Atahan walked into the ANZ Bank at 7 Macquarie Place, Sydney. Armed with his trademark tools of a sawn-off rifle and pistol, he 'withdrew' $10,000, which was handed over by terrified bank staff.

The hold-up was trouble free and, once Atahan was back on the street, he could simply have melted into the passers-by outside. But, amazingly, he headed next door into the State Bank and, again at gunpoint, held up the bank staff for $9000.

This additional thrill would have been more than enough for most criminals, but not Atahan. His adrenaline flowing, he walked into the nearby Commonwealth Bank at 200 George Street. This northern area of the city, near Circular Quay, represented the heart of the commercial area, making it ideal for a bank robber, with plenty of targets close together. There were also plenty of risks. Atahan's luck was not everlasting.

Two young uniformed police constables from Phillip Street Police Station had responded to the first alarm at the ANZ Bank. Accompanied by an employee, they patrolled the area in the vicinity of the bank, searching for the offender. Their observations were keen and they spotted Atahan entering the Commonwealth Bank. They called for extra police assistance and the bank was soon surrounded and secured. This, however, resulted in a hostage situation, when Atahan realised he was trapped inside.

Atahan discharged the pistol into the ceiling of the bank to settle down anybody who was thinking of being a hero. The bullet narrowly missed Stephen Lamb, a 23-year-old bank clerk who was standing near the gunman.

The terrified bank officer was forced to operate the bank switchboard as a conduit between Atahan and police negotiators who had arrived in their special van. The vehicle was like an armoured car, bullet resistant and fitted out with mobile telephones, loudhailers, radios, both police and commercial, as well as reference maps. Facilities for tea and coffee making were also available as hostage situations could drag on for many hours.

Atahan was becoming increasingly excited and indecisive as his confidence began to desert him. He made a demand for an escape vehicle to be brought to the front of the bank. But before police could act on this development, he suddenly emerged from the bank, surrounded by five hostages. The hostages had been ordered to stick close to him, each of them with one hand placed on his head. Atahan controlled the group by holding a .32 calibre Browning pistol to the head of the bank manager, Graham Stewart. Any sudden movement and he would shoot the manager.

The public had been warned by police to vacate the area around the bank and one member of the community, in his haste, left his blue Datsun sedan abandoned in Bridge Street with the keys in the ignition. Atahan forced his hostages into the car and ordered the manager to drive.

The Datsun headed east towards Bondi, with an increasing number of police cars following. Suddenly it changed direction and the convoy travelled back through the city, across the Sydney Harbour Bridge and into Mosman. Atahan had switched on the car radio to monitor news bulletins and any relevant information regarding his circumstances. Instead, he heard the radio announcer describing him as 'a lunatic on the loose'.

Atahan directed the manager to drive towards his home turf at Manly, where he ordered him to stop outside a public phone box. He forced one of the hostages to ring his prostitute girlfriend and arrange a meeting with her at Queenscliff Beach.

The young woman kept the appointment, and she too was dragged into the overcrowded car. Atahan released one of the panic-stricken hostages before he and his hostages continued on their journey around Sydney's northern suburbs.

The gunman was desperate and seemed to be losing the plot. The hostages were also terrified, not knowing when their captor would sacrifice them for his freedom. The car was crowded and they had been held for some hours.

POLICE MAKE THEIR MOVE

The police contingent had now been reinforced with members of the Special Weapons Operations Squad (SWOS) and a decision was made to block the fugitive's car. The Spit Bridge, spanning Middle Harbour, is an old style, opening bridge, designed to allow shipping into the inner harbour. The police ordered that the bridge be opened to halt Atahan's progress. The red traffic lights came on, and the bridge slowly opened. This brought traffic to a standstill, trapping Atahan and his hostages in the lanes of cars waiting to cross the bridge.

Police negotiators left their van and approached Atahan, attempting to communicate with him. He shunned their efforts and turned up the volume of the car radio to drown out their voices. He then ordered the bank manager to drive the

Datsun over the median strip and travel back towards Manly. Hostage Stephen Lamb described what happened next:

> *A police car drove right in front of us and forced us to stop—we were completely surrounded and there were guns everywhere. I was seated in the middle in the back. He still had a gun at the manager's head. A policeman, Detective Senior Constable Steven Canellis, was crouching down with a gun pointed at the offender and trying to talk to him reasonably. The offender took his gun away from the manager's head and pointed it at the policeman. He said, 'You're fucked now', and fired.*

Detective Sergeant John Nagle, a marksman attached to the SWOS team, had positioned himself at the rear of the hostage car and had a clear sight of the gunman. When he saw Atahan shoot his colleague, Nagle shouted in a loud voice, 'Hostages in the back—don't move, don't move'. Then he pulled the trigger on his M16 Armalite rifle and shot the offender.

Their ordeal over, the hostages were released from the car, shaken and slightly injured by flying glass, but with their lives no longer threatened. Psychologically, however, only time would reveal their injuries.

OFFICER DOWN

Atahan was dead and Detective Canellis was seriously wounded. A .32 calibre bullet had entered the centre of the policeman's face, travelled down through his throat and lodged below his right shoulder.

Fatal Odyssey

An ambulance had been called, but the traffic was so thick that the emergency vehicle met with plenty of obstacles. Canellis's life expectancy at that point was measured in minutes. But miracles do happen. Skilful, medical hands were nearby.

Dr Carl Hughes, a general practitioner, specially trained in emergency treatment of gunshot injury victims, had also been caught in the traffic banked up at the Spit Bridge. Dr Hughes was the commander of the St John Ambulance gunshot wounds clinic. His expertise and prompt attendance to Canellis saved the policeman's life. Later, at the Coronial Inquest into the death of Hakki Atahan, the doctor related:

> *I was very concerned that the policeman might have had brain injuries and, of course I was worried about his breathing. Blood was pouring from his nose and mouth and my initial concern was the first-aid principle of putting him in a situation where blood would drain away from his throat, because I was terribly concerned that if he became unconscious and was allowed to lie on his back, he would have certainly died.*

When the ambulance reached the scene, the doctor advised the crew to transport the injured detective to the Royal North Shore Hospital rather than the closer Manly Hospital, because specialised treatment would be available there.

The time was now 8pm, some five hours had elapsed since Atahan began his fatal adventure. Police cars, ambulances, television and press vehicles had formed a procession, led by the offender. The police helicopter Polair hovered overhead, maintaining surveillance.

CORONIAL INQUIRY

On 12 July 1984, a Coronial Inquest into the death of Hakki Bahadi Atahan was held in Sydney before Coroner Mrs M. Sleeman. She praised the bravery and calmness shown by bank employees, both during the armed robberies and later, when they were taken hostage. Dr Hughes received special mention and congratulations for his treatment of the seriously wounded Detective Senior Constable Stephen Francis Canellis of the NSW Police Armed Hold-Up Squad. The coroner found that:

> On the 31st day of January 1984, in Manly Road, Seaforth, near the Spit Bridge, Hakki Bahadi Atahan died from the effects of bullet wounds to the head and chest inflicted by police officers acting in the course of their duty, such killing being justifiable homicide.

A POLICE OFFICER IS REWARDED

Steve Canellis survived the shooting by Atahan and was commended by Her Majesty the Queen for his brave conduct. He was awarded the Commendation for Brave Conduct Medal and the Police Commissioner's Commendation for courage.

Steve has since retired from the NSW Police Force. Unfortunately, to this day, he still carries in his body the bullet that Atahan fired at him as it was considered too dangerous to remove. Steve and I meet occasionally and I value his company even more now when I consider that he too could have been a subject of a Coronial Inquiry resulting from that 31 January 1984 'fatal odyssey'.

CHAPTER THIRTEEN

THE HITCHHIKERS' TRAP

Darryl Stanley Collins was an impetuous youth who obtained satisfaction from being involved as an informant or as an offender, and confessed to minor crimes that he had committed. Most of his crimes, however, were imaginary. Collins just liked hanging around police stations.

Collins was 15 years of age and it came as no surprise to me when, on 9 January 1974, he walked into the Cronulla Police Station, where I was then Detective Sergeant in Charge, with another one of his stories. Or was it? Collins complained that he had been raped by two men who alleged they were police officers.

About 10pm the previous night, 8 January 1974, Collins claimed that he was hitchhiking along the Kingsway, in Cronulla, the main highway leading to the southern Sydney beach suburb of Cronulla. A white Ford panel van containing two men, stopped and offered him a lift to near his home at Caringbah, a distance of about three kilometres.

The youth accepted the offer and entered the vehicle, where he sat between the driver and the passenger. Instead of being allowed to leave the vehicle near his home, however, he was driven to an isolated area at the rear of the Sutherland Hospital. There, the men introduced themselves as detectives from the Drug Squad.

They informed Collins that they had been assigned to investigate drug offences in the Cronulla area and they produced what appeared to be a police identification certificate and a pistol. Collins was ordered into the back of the panel van, which was fitted out with a mattress and told that he was to be searched for drugs.

The two men then forcibly undressed Collins at gunpoint and removed from his wrist a gold bracelet engraved with his name. The piece of jewellery was thrown onto the floor of the vehicle. Each man then took turns to indecently assault and sodomise Collins. The youth was subjected to these indignities for over a period of one hour. Then he was allowed to dress and was driven to near his home. The vehicle was hastily driven away, leaving Collins with no chance of obtaining the registration number.

The district government medical officer was located at Sutherland and Collins was taken there by police for a medical examination. The result surprised the police. It confirmed Collins' story that he had been sexually interfered with. However, because of the victim's past history, the police could not overlook the possibility that Collins had been a consenting party to sodomy under entirely different circumstances than those he had related to them. He may well have concocted this incredible story for the purpose of involving himself in a police investigation. Nevertheless, descriptions of the suspects and their motor vehicle were circulated for the information of all police.

ANOTHER VICTIM

About 6.30pm on 14 July 1974, 16-year-old Richard John Lynch was hitchhiking in the Kingsway when he was offered a ride by two men in a similar vehicle to the one described by Darryl Collins. The youth told the two men he was travelling to Sutherland, approximately 10 kilometres away, and they agreed to drive him there.

Lynch entered the vehicle and sat between the two men, but instead of being driven to Sutherland, he was driven to bushland at the Royal National Park. He was told by the men that they were both going to rape him. The terrified youth scrambled over the front seat into the back of the panel van in an attempt to escape, but found that the door could not be opened from the inside.

With one man holding the youth down, they took turns to sexually assault the boy. The attacks were vile and disgusting and lasted for almost an hour. Lynch was forced from the car and left in the bushland as the offenders drove away. He walked about two kilometres to the home of a friend where he related what had happened.

The matter was reported to the police at Sutherland and, once again, following a medical examination, the allegations were confirmed and supported. Lynch had been raped.

Richard Lynch, although unable to supply a registration number, was able to give police a detailed description of the offenders. That was circulated for the information of all police:

> *Wanted for indecent assault male—first offender, the driver of the vehicle, 26 years old, 5ft 10ins [175cm], solid build, suntanned complexion, short dark brown hair going grey, rough and dirty appearance with several days growth of beard.*
>
> *The second offender, about 25 years old, 5ft 8ins [172cm], medium to flabby build, fair complexion, round face, shoulder length light brown hair, well spoken and neatly dressed.*
>
> *The vehicle described as a 1968 Ford Falcon panel van, white colour with the tailgate painted black, having an air intake scoop mounted on the bonnet and rear-vision mirrors on each front mudguard.*

Lynch noticed that the interior of the vehicle had a three-speed gear floor-change, a purple, furry cover across the top of the dashboard, an eight-track stereo cartridge player below the dashboard on the driver's side, three additional gauges fitted to the instrument panel, dark blue curtains over all the rear windows with a mattress and blankets in the rear cabin. He also noticed a gold bracelet hanging from the interior rear-vision mirror.

The type of crime and the description of the offenders and their vehicle matched the information supplied by Darryl Collins. Could the gold bracelet hanging from the rear-vision mirror belong to Collins? Was it a sign of a conquest, a notch on the gun?

Special patrols were maintained in the Cronulla area by police in plainclothes and unmarked cars with attention being directed at youths hitchhiking. There was no sign of the offenders or their vehicle.

ONE TIME TOO MANY

On 29 July 1974, the inquiries turned in favour of the police, but not before another youth was brutally and sexually assaulted. A third victim came to Cronulla Police Station. This time, however, he was able to supply the registration number of the offenders' vehicle.

The victim was Peter English, a 16-year-old school student who was accompanied to the station by his father. He related to me how he had been subjected to three hours of horrifying indignities. So shamed was he by the attack that he confided with his parents and elder brother for over 24 hours before it was decided he should report the matter to the police.

There is no better way to relate what happened to Peter than by reproducing the report made on that day:

About 7.45pm on Saturday, the 27th July 1974, I attended a dance held at The Last Picture Show, Cronulla. At some time between 11.45pm and 12.15am, I left the dance with the intention of hitchhiking to my home, which is about a mile and a half from Cronulla. I went to the Kingsway, Cronulla, outside Cronulla Police Station and commenced to hitchhike for a ride. I waited for about five minutes and then I commenced to walk along the Kingsway towards Caringbah.

When I had gone about 20 yards, a white panel van containing two men stopped alongside of me and the man sitting in the passenger's seat got out and held the door open and indicated for me to get into the vehicle. I got into the panel van and sat alongside of the driver and then the passenger got in and sat alongside of me.

The driver I would describe as being 25 to 30 years old, about 5ft 8ins [172cm] tall, solid build, about 13 stone [82 kilograms], dark untidy hair, roughly shaven, gold fillings in his teeth, a wide nose, smelt of alcohol and was wearing a purple T-shirt and shoes. The passenger was about 28 years old, noticeably shorter than the driver, medium build, light brown straight hair with a long fringe combed across his forehead, glassy eyes, thin nose and clean shaven. He was wearing mid-brown long trousers, matching jacket, light-coloured shirt and shoes. He was quietly spoken, but the driver spoke coarsely.

When I entered the panel van, the driver said, 'Where are you going?' I said, 'To Gannons Road.' He muttered something to the passenger, but I couldn't understand what was said. The driver said to me, 'Where have you been tonight?' I said, 'To The Last Picture Show.' He said, 'What's on there? The flicks or a dance?' I said, 'Some groups were on.' He said, 'What sort of night did you have?' I said, 'Not very successful. I didn't meet any nice chicks.' The driver said, 'Oh, you missed out.' He and the passenger then began to laugh.

At this time we were in the Kingsway approaching the street where I wanted to get out and I said, 'You can let me off just past the intersection.' The driver said, 'I'll just drive you around the block,' and I agreed because it would be closer to my home.

The driver drove into Caringbah Road which was pretty dark and he said to me, 'Have you had anything to drink tonight?' I said, 'No.' He then said, 'Have you smoked any grass?' I said, 'No.' The driver said, 'You really think that you haven't smoked any dope tonight?'

The driver then told me that he and the passenger were police from the Special Drug Squad and said, 'How would you like to be taken home to your parents in handcuffs and your parents told that we had arrested their son for smoking dope?' I put my hands out and said, 'Go right ahead because I haven't been.'

The driver said to the passenger, 'Have you got a spare set of handcuffs around?' The passenger said, 'I'll have a look', and he just looked around the glove box and the cabin of the vehicle. The driver said, 'We've got a few more things to check before we take you.'

I asked them for their identification and the driver took a wallet from his trousers pocket and pulled out what looked like a licence. I couldn't see any names and he just put it back in his pocket. He then said, 'What's your name and address?' and the passenger took a small black book from the glove box and started to write.

I was very scared as both men were older and bigger than me and had been using obscene language and being late in the night I could not see any other person or motor vehicles around. The men also used threatening language when they began to ask me the names of people I knew that smoked 'grass' and they suggested that if I did not tell them, they would push my face in and then ask me again. They began to pressure me for names and I became very scared that they would harm me if I didn't give them some names so I mentioned two fellows that I know from school. These names were written down in the book.

The driver then took from the glove box a small bottle and he took a pill out. He said, 'If you have one of these and you've smoked dope within the last three weeks, you're going *to be really sick'. He handed me the pill and told me to take it. Even though I doubted they were police, I was really scared that if I didn't take the pill, they would force me to, so I swallowed it. I began to shake, but it was not through the pill, it was because I was so nervous and scared.*

The driver said, 'We want to search you now. Get over into the back and we'll check your shoes, socks and pants.' I climbed over into the back and the driver climbed over and started to look through my shoes. He then felt along the seams of my pants and he said, 'Take your pants off and I'll check around the top.' I thought then that they might be police because he seemed to know how to search a person. I removed my trousers and the driver searched them and found nothing.

I knew that we were coming to a point in the interview that would be very embarrassing for the young man to relate, even to a male police officer. I called for a coffee break. We spoke about everyday matters, his schooling, his hobbies and his life in general. English became more relaxed, and I felt that when we continued with his harrowing revelations, he might be more at ease.

I was about to put my trousers back on when the driver grabbed them and threw them to the back of the panel van. He said, 'I want to search your underpants.' He felt inside my underpants and grabbed hold of my penis. He then started to run his hands under my shirt and over my chest. I was petrified and thought that he was a sex maniac and I feared for my life. Then he grabbed my penis again and wouldn't let go. I was terrified and thought that if they didn't get what they wanted, they would drive to somewhere like the national park and kill me.

English went on to describe how the two men then forcibly raped him in turn, not once, but each three times. The driver returned to the front seat and began to move the car. The victim had visions running through his head of being driven to isolated bushland, or to the country where he would be killed, and his body dumped. He had in fact been driven to the sand hills near Cronulla High School at Wanda Beach. There, the two men violently abused English and submitted him to further acts of sodomy.

I really thought then that I was to be killed, but they drove me to near my home and let me out of the panel van. It was then about 2.50am on the Sunday, nearly three hours after I had been picked up. As soon as I got home, I woke my father and told him what had happened.

I left inside the panel van a blue biro pen, a pair of purple jockey underpants and a pair of socks which are a goldish colour with a pair of blue feet embroidered on each sock.

The young man's description of the panel van was similar in all respects to that involved in the two previous attacks. I wondered how a youth, so brutally assaulted, could have the presence of mind to remember and relate such a complete description of his abductors. He was, in my mind, quite special

A medical examination of English revealed that he had been most viciously and savagely sodomised. Bruises on his body attesting to his unwillingness to be a consenting party.

POLICE CLOSE IN

A check on the registration number revealed that the vehicle was a white 1968 Ford Falcon panel van owned by a Barry Clarke of 31 Liney Street, Campsie. Police surveillance was immediately placed on the premises. At 5.30pm on 29 July 1974, the vehicle was seen to arrive.

I took a couple of detectives with me and we hurried to the address. The surveillance crew was still in position. The panel van had not moved. Police covered the front and rear entrances of the house. When we knocked on the front door, the suspect attempted to leave by the back door. An old trick, but one that is very, very worn out. He was arrested.

Barry Clarke proved to be the person each victim referred to as 'the driver', and his bedroom was searched. On his bed were the underpants and socks that had been left in the panel van by English. In a bedside table drawer, the notebook referred to by the victim was found, also a replica .38 calibre revolver. Behind a wardrobe, the searchers found a fully loaded .22 calibre rifle.

The offender's vehicle was searched and Peter English's biro and a bottle of pills were found in the glove box. A gold chain bracelet, engraved 'Darryl' was found hanging from the interior rear-vision mirror. This was later identified as the one owned by the first victim, Darryl Collins.

Clarke was briefly interviewed at his home and he implicated the second offender as being Kim Coulson Cathro, who resided with him, but at that time was at the Sydney GPO, where he was employed as a switchboard operator. Police were dispatched to that location and a short time later, Cathro was in police custody.

Clarke was taken to Cronulla Police Station, and it seemed ironic that when driving along the Kingsway, Darryl Collins, the first victim, was seen hitchhiking.

Barry Clarke proved to be identical with Barry William Johnson, alias Kenneth William Pallister, with 15 entries on his criminal history sheet for offences mainly of dishonesty. He was born in 1944, unmarried, and had had no association with any relative for over seven years. Clarke was a labourer employed by a motor spare parts company at Arncliffe in Sydney's inner south and, according to all his work mates, a willing worker and a rough, manly type.

The second offender was Kim Coulson Cathro, also unmarried. He too was born in 1944. Cathro had no previous brushes with the law. He was an effeminate type and had been raised by his aunty who was the owner of the house where he and Clarke lived.

In August 1969, both offenders went through a form of marriage that was attended and witnessed by other homosexuals. Since that date, both men had lived together.

Towards the end of 1973, Clarke began to experience periods where he would tire of Cathro's company and it was then, at Clarke's instigation, that a routine was devised to commit acts of sodomy on youths found hitchhiking. The Cronulla area was selected because of the large numbers of prospective victims who hitchhiked around this beach resort.

How many victims had been subjected to this violence was a subject for contemplation. Maybe others had been too embarrassed to report their violation to police.

THE CHARGES

Both offenders were charged at Cronulla Police Station on 29 July 1974, each with three charges of buggery, committed on Darryl Collins, Richard Lynch and Peter English. Three further charges were made against Clarke and Cathro: indecent assault on a male person, assume designation of a police officer and possession of a firearm.

On the 22 August 1974, both prisoners appeared before His Honour Judge Barry Thorley at the Sydney District Court and pleaded guilty to the three buggery charges. Clarke informed the judge that he had become a homosexual while serving a prison sentence in 1966, when he was forcibly subjected to acts of sodomy by fellow prisoners. This was rejected by the judge as being an excuse, not a reason.

Both offenders were condemned as having committed some of the most disgraceful, animal acts that His Honour had ever known in all his years as a judge. Both prisoners collapsed in the dock when Clarke was sentenced to 15 years' hard labour and Cathro to 10 years' hard labour. Later appeals by both men to the Court of Criminal Appeal were dismissed and their convictions confirmed.

Lynch and English had been cured of hitchhiking They had learned the dangers the hard way. Collins was different. He saw nothing wrong with the practice, probably believing the experience was simply a one-off misadventure.

CHAPTER FOURTEEN

THE SCENT
OF A CRIME

Over half a century ago, NSW Police officers aiming to become detectives would sit for the Detectives Designation Examination. This test comprised several subjects, including one named 'powers of observation'.

A crime scene was prepared by the examiners in a special room. Each applicant would be given five minutes to peruse the setting, search for clues, gather evidence and then submit a comprehensive, written report on his or her determinations.

Invariably, the night before the examination, a leak would develop and an 'anonymous' phone call to an aspirant would simply state, 'It's a murder scene', or 'It's a safe robbery'. Of course, the quiz masters soon became aware of the tip-off and used it to their advantage by remodelling the display with fewer or more clues on the day of the test.

I recall one would-be detective spending an undue amount of time searching under a table. When asked by an instructor if he was alright, the candidate replied, 'I can't find the train ticket that should be here.' Needless to say, he failed the examination.

Police also learned from this examination that each real-life crime scene is a display of clues, exhibits and what has been left by the offender for the police to reconstruct the crime, and nothing could be taken or presumed from what lay in front of them. The investigator's eyes and mind had to co-ordinate to find an often elusive piece of evidence. Elusive maybe, but according to forensic scientist Professor Edmond Locard's theory of transference, the evidence is always there.

AUNTY ELSIE

Elsie Elizabeth Miles was a frail, 84-year-old widow living alone in a modest cottage in residential Culwalla Street, South Hurstville, in Sydney's south. In August 1977, she was admitted to St George Hospital where she underwent minor surgery for a hernia problem.

Upon discharge Elsie Miles returned home and was visited regularly by her neighbours, who watched over her. Her recovery to normal health was progressing satisfactorily.

At 5.30pm on 29 September 1977, an elderly neighbour, Martha Rosten, called to visit Mrs Miles. The front door was open and, as was her usual practice, Mrs Rosten entered the house. She was confronted in the hallway by a young man. Startled, she asked the man, 'Who are you?'

He replied, 'Bernie Simpson. I'm a friend. Have you heard Aunty Elsie talking about me? I live at Rooty Hill and I came to see her today. She's been in hospital.'

The Scent of a Crime

Mrs Rosten asked Simpson, 'Are you staying with her?'

'Just for tonight. She's asleep on the lounge now,' he said.

The neighbour could see her friend lying on a sofa in the back room with a shawl wrapped around her head. As she moved closer to Elsie, the young man knelt down beside the prone woman and, lifting her head, said, 'Why have you wrapped your shawl around your head, Aunty?' as he removed the piece of clothing from her head.

Mrs Rosten saw that the old lady had her eyes closed and was motionless.

'She looks sick,' she exclaimed. 'I'll have to ring for a doctor. I'll ring from my place.'

Mrs Rosten rang Elsie Miles' GP, Dr Raymond Wilson of Blakehurst, and then returned to her friend's home. Bernard Simpson had gone. The neighbour did not consider this to be anything other than a lack of concern on Simpson's behalf.

Upon examination, Dr Wilson pronounced that Elsie Miles was dead. He noticed a superficial laceration to her left temple that may have been caused by a fall. He considered that the old lady had died of natural causes and was prepared to issue a death certificate stating that her heart had failed. The police at Kogarah Station were contacted to arrange removal of the body to the city morgue.

On their arrival, the police made the usual observations of the inside of the house. Contents were scattered about the bedroom, but this, said the doctor, was the usual condition in which the house was maintained.

The deceased was dressed in a blue frock, cardigan, stockings and slippers and had a beret on her head. She was still wearing a pair of spectacles and there was her walking stick alongside her on the settee. There were several small holes, possibly caused by moths, in Mrs Miles' cardigan. Police noticed a number of small, star-shaped blemishes on her chest, similar to scars left after the removal of a mole or small cyst. Apart from the minor head laceration, Mrs Miles had no other penetrating injuries on her body.

But the scent wasn't right. Why had Bernard Simpson not remained at the scene? There was more to this death than first met the eye. The police might well end up with egg on their faces, but the circumstances just weren't as clear and straight forward as they might seem. A crime scene was set up. Dr Wilson was prevailed upon to withhold issuing a death certificate and instead, the police requested a post mortem.

The usual procedures were followed—a crime scene examination was made of the house in search of clues. This was not a police in-house, play-acting test, but the real thing. Training was now turned into practice for the two new detectives who were called to the scene.

The government pathologist attended the scene and made a quick external examination of the deceased before her removal to the morgue. There, a complete post-mortem examination would be made of Elsie Miles.

THE POST MORTEM

The results of the post mortem were both surprising and enlightening. Apart from the abrasions to the left side of her head, Elsie Miles had suffered fractures to four ribs and puncture wounds to her heart and lungs. These injuries were adjacent to the star-shaped marks the police noticed on her chest. The so-called 'moth holes' in Elsie Miles' cardigan lined up perfectly with the marks.

The crime scene examination had uncovered several exhibits, including fingerprints, hairs and fibres. A Phillips-head screwdriver on a table near where the deceased had been found puzzled the investigators. Old people of Elsie Miles' age usually don't dabble with such tools. The post mortem provided the answer to its presence.

The screwdriver's head matched identically with the star-shaped marks on the old lady's chest. The conclusion of the pathologist was that the deceased had been stabbed seven times with the screwdriver, thus delivering the internal injuries. The skin of the old lady was so pliant and tractable that it formed a sheath around the shaft of the murder weapon, allowing entry into the body without tearing the skin. On each withdrawal of the screwdriver, the malleable skin returned to its normal shape.

SUSPECT INTERVIEWED

It didn't prove difficult to establish who Bernard Simpson was and where he resided. Bernard Richard Simpson was born on 23 September 1951 and resided with his wife and two children in York Street, Fairfield. He was employed as a patrolman with the State Transit Authority.

Later that night, police went to Simpson's home and spoke to him. He admitted to having visited his 'aunty' earlier that evening, but knew nothing about her death.

He was conveyed to Kogarah Police Station where a typed, recorded interview was conducted. There, Simpson had a change of heart, his conscience was now in control. He wanted to tell the police what had occurred. Some of the questions put to Simpson, and his answers, revealed what had happened:

Q: How long have you known Elsie Elizabeth Miles?

A: About eight years. I met her through friends of mine, related to her…her brother Arthur Hooper and his wife Mrs Hooper, and their daughter Anne Hooper.

Q: Do you know where Mrs Miles lives?

A: Yes. At 14 Culwulla Street, South Hurstville. She has only been living there for about six years. I have visited her about three times.

Q: Did you visit her home yesterday?

A: Yes. I thought of Elsie, wondering what her condition was, concerned about her being in hospital. I decided to ring her up. When she answered the phone, she sounded very depressed and lonely. I felt sorry for her and asked her if she would like me to visit her because I was not doing anything at the time and felt that I could cheer her up. She said that she would be very pleased if I could come over and I said that I would be over by about five o'clock or so. I caught a train to Hurstville and walked to her house.

The Scent of a Crime

The key was in the front door and I knew that people were calling in all the time to check on her. At the door I called 'Elsie'—this would be about 5pm. She didn't answer. I looked at both bedrooms as I walked in and proceeded up the hallway, where I found her on the sofa.

Q: What happened after that?

A: I greeted her and sat down in a chair at the head of the sofa. She told me about her condition and she didn't look well. We had a conversation for about half an hour about family and work and things like that. All this time she was lying on the sofa. I spoke to her about my financial worries in regard to the purchasing of a house. She then began to talk about her brother Arthur relating to a woman who was handling her money and Arthur was taking the side of this woman, and I took Arthur's side and she and I began to argue and it became a heated argument over this matter.

I can't tell you word for word what was said between her and myself because I was getting very angry. She argued that this woman, I don't know her name, was using her money and I took Arthur's side defending him as I believed Arthur not her. We continued to argue. She was sitting on the sofa with a stick by her right side, she grabbed the stick and swung it at me whilst she was still on the sofa. As she swung the stick at me, she began to rise from the sofa and the stick caught me on the right side of the face.

I grabbed the walking stick from her hand, I don't know which hand she was holding it in and she was sitting up. I hit her on the left side of the head near the temple, twice in quick succession with the curved bit of the walking stick which is near the straight part of the stick.

Q: What did you do then?

A: I recoiled in shock and covered her face with a blue shawl which was on the sofa with her. I was very angry with her and I retaliated with the walking stick to hurt her for what she had done to me and said. I ran to the front of the house to see if there were any valuables I could take—money or anything. I then heard footsteps outside the front of the house, someone was coming—I wanted to get out of the house. It was a woman, I have never seen her before, but she told me that she was one of Elsie's neighbours.

Q: When this woman left the house, did you enter any rooms in the house?

A: I went straight out, when she left. I walked down the hill towards Woniora Road and got a train. I went to Redfern and then got a train to Fairfield, got off there and picked up my car and went and picked up the kids and took them home.

Q: Do you agree that last night you told me that you were nowhere near Elsie Miles' house yesterday?

A: I lied when I told you that—I had a guilt feeling, I was trying to figure things out—after I did that to her, I thought the opportunity was there to go through the house to see what money and valuables I could take.

Q: An examination of Mrs Miles showed that she had been stabbed several times. What do you know about that?

A: I was in a rage, yes. I could have done it. I deeply regret my actions and I only hope that there was something that I could have done to prevent this terrible thing from happening. I can't forgive myself.

Bernard Simpson seemed to have only one motive for this murder—greed. He wanted money for nothing from Mrs Miles.

ARREST AND TRIAL

On 30 September 1977, Bernard Richard Simpson was charged at Kogarah Police Station with the murder of Elsie Elizabeth Miles. He appeared at the Central Court of Petty Sessions, where he was committed to stand trial.

On 23 June 1978, he was found guilty by a jury at his trial in Sydney's Central Criminal Court. Before Simpson was sentenced, he made a statement from the dock:

I had no reason to kill Mrs Miles and would not benefit from her death in any manner whatsoever. I am sincerely full of sorrow and remorse for her passing and trust that she is resting in peace and suffered no pain when she died.

His Honour Justice Cross sentenced Simpson to penal servitude for life.

The 'powers of observation' proved positive in solving this crime by police noticing the seven, small star-shaped scars. The two young detectives had placed their training lectures into real-life examination of a crime scene. They could have been wrong, but they weren't. The scent of a crime was certainly there.

CHAPTER FIFTEEN

THE LION'S DEN

A solicitor once quoted to me a proverb that could well be applied to the main player in this story: 'He who escapes from the lion's den should not return to retrieve his hat'.

THE ARREST

On 14 March 1979, Raymond Bowers Cessna and Timothy William Lycett Milner were arrested by Sydney detectives in possession of 137.5 kilograms of Indian hemp. The substance was in the form of 110,000 buddha sticks and, because of the large commercial quantity, an indictable charge was laid under Section 21(1) (a) of the *Poisons Act 1966*. The determination of such a charge was mandatory before a judge and jury in the NSW Supreme Court. The street value of the drugs was estimated at $2.5 million.

Both offenders were aged in their forties and appeared on 15 March 1979 at the Central Court of Petty Sessions before

Mr M. Farquhar, the NSW Chief Stipendiary Magistrate. Raymond Cessna was a businessman residing on the lower north shore of Sydney and he was granted bail in the sum of $20,000. Timothy Milner was a British national and a citizen of the world, with no fixed place of abode in Sydney. He was refused bail and remanded in custody.

Both men appeared on two further occasions before the same magistrate, with bail subsequently being granted to both in the sum of $20,000. The defendants were represented by Mr Bruce Miles, solicitor from the law firm of Morgan Ryan and Brock. They were remanded to appear at the same court on 15 May 1979. On that day, a suitable hearing date would be set, when evidence would be taken during the lower court committal proceedings.

AN EARLY HEARING

On 15 May 1979, again before Mr Farquhar, both men appeared at the Central Court of Petty Sessions. The arresting police were not in attendance as only a hearing date was to be set that day. However, both defendants were re-charged by the magistrate under Section 21(1) (a) of the Poisons Act, without reference to Section 45A(4), which meant that the matter could now be dealt with in the lower court. No consultation was held with the arresting police officers in respect to this alteration.

At 12.30pm, the charge case of possession of a commercial quantity of drugs against the two offenders was moved from the No. 1 court to the smaller, less public No. 5 court. The magistrate altered the estimated street value on the records to read from $2.5 million to 'of some value'. He then proceeded to deal with the matter summarily.

Cessna and Milner pleaded guilty to the fresh, lesser charges and, as the arresting police were not in attendance at the court, the brief facts taken from the arrest sheet were accepted as evidence by the magistrate.

Milner was sentenced to 18 months' hard labour, with a non-parole period of eight months. He would be deported to England at the expiry of the non-parole period. Cessna was remanded on bail to 24 May 1979 for sentence. On that date, he was fined $1000 and required to enter into a recognisance to be of good behaviour for a period of 12 months. Mr Farquhar was again the magistrate and he retired from the magistracy the following day.

Mr Farquhar's decision to deal with the drug charges in such a manner resulted in considerable publicity and great disapproval by the arresting police. Whatever the disquiet, the case had been finalised. The deed had been done.

Upon Mr Farquhar's retirement from the bench, Mr C.R. Briese was appointed Chairman of the Bench of Stipendiary Magistrates. In June 1979, as a result of the controversy following the Cessna–Milner court case, Mr Briese forwarded a letter to the Under Secretary of Justice, Mr T.W. Haines, which stated, among other things:

> *I cannot say what was in the mind of Mr Farquhar when he agreed to deal with the charges summarily. As the law now stands, it was legally permissible for him to deal with the charges summarily. However, after consultation with my colleagues at Central Court, I have to report that in our experience, it is not the practice and never has been the practice by any of the*

Magistrates at Central Court to deal summarily with matters of this kind. There can be no doubt that matters of this kind should never be dealt with summarily for, even supposing the drug to have little or no value, one cannot speak for the mind of the person buying it.

THE FIRST POLICE INQUIRY

The handling of the Cessna–Milner case, as it was now known, continued to receive high public exposure. Mr J.T. Lees had been appointed Commissioner of the NSW Police Force and he directed that a police inquiry should be carried out into the circumstances surrounding the alteration of the charges against Cessna and Milner from indictable to summary matters.

Timothy Milner had been deported from Australia by the time of the police inquiry, and his whereabouts were unknown. Raymond Cessna refused to be interviewed.

The inquiry showed that the magistrate, Mr Farquhar, had taken upon himself the responsibility of determining the case in a summary manner, despite the strong objections made by the police prosecutor on that day. The arresting police were also distressed that a strong indictable matter, bringing with it a lengthy jail sentence on conviction, was dealt with in the manner in which it was finalised, that they were never consulted.

The then Solicitor General for New South Wales, Mr G.T.A. Sullivan, QC, prepared a report following the police inquiry. Although critical of the behaviour of Cessna and Milner and their solicitor Mr Miles, and of Mr Farquhar, there appeared insufficient admissible evidence to sustain prosecution against them to pervert the course of justice.

That would seem to be the end of the matter. But there would be more.

THE ROYAL COMMISSION

During the 1980s, government and public concern was alerted to the alleged, unlawful interception by police of a series of telephone conversations. Although the intercepts were being used as a crime-fighting device and levelled only against criminals, the action was totally illegal and in contravention of the Telecommunications Act.

On 6 May 1985, pursuant to a Letters Patent issued by the Governor General of Australia and the governors of New South Wales and Victoria, a Royal Commission of Inquiry Into Alleged Telephone Interceptions was established. His Honour Mr Justice Donald G. Stewart was appointed as the sole Royal Commissioner.

One reference to be considered and examined by Justice Stewart was the Cessna–Milner matter. Those arrests had eventuated through information obtained from illegal telephone interceptions that were placed on the telephone service of Raymond Bowers Cessna.

A photograph taken of Cessna's solicitor, Morgan Ryan, meeting with Magistrate Murray Farquhar in Centennial Park also found its way from the NSW state parliament to the bench of the Royal Commissioner. As a result of the illegal phone taps that remained on Cessna's phone after his arrest, it was ascertained that Cessna had been contacted by his solicitor, asking him to make himself present but out of sight at the Centennial Park meeting. This was to prove to Cessna that the solicitor could speak to Farquhar inappropriately. The irresistible inference drawn from this meeting was that it was conducted so openly as to allow observations to be made by Cessna to confirm in his mind that 'something could be done to assist him' in his forthcoming court case.

Members of the NSW Police Intelligence Unit photographed the meeting, but at the time of the Royal Commission, neither the photos nor the negatives could be located. The then Premier of the New South Wales, Mr Nick Greiner, declined to reveal the source of his print, claiming parliamentary privilege.

On 30 April 1986, the Royal Commissioner presented his final report. Justice Stewart found that a number of matters remained unresolved and he directed some of those tasks to be further examined by appropriate bodies. Ten such tasks were directed to the then NSW Police Commissioner, John Avery. The Commissioner's Task Force was established for this purpose and I was appointed as the leader.

THE TASK FORCE INQUIRY

The conclusions of the Royal Commissioner were factual, according to the civil standard of proof. Whether a criminal standard of proof existed would be considered following the investigation and recommendation of the task force. Criminal proof, of course, was more demanding than civil. Proof beyond reasonable doubt was necessary.

The investigation was also '...to make further recomendations as to the method of enforcement of the criminal law and the legislative and administrative changes that are necessary and the nature of the information disclosed at the Royal Commission of the possible commission of criminal offences that warrants further investigation'.

One of those tasks was a reinvestigation of the Cessna–Milner matter. Additional evidence was now available. That of the photographed meeting between Farquhar and solicitor Morgan Ryan, which indicated Ryan's closeness to Farquhar at a time when he was determining the solicitor's case.

The Royal Commissioner had reached two conclusions in relation to that inquiry, and these were conveyed to the task force.

1. Ryan acted for Cessna although he did not appear in court and his relationship with Cessna was not a proper relationship as between solicitor and client. For some reason not disclosed by the evidence, he was prepared to go to inordinate lengths to ensure his client was dealt with on a less serious charge. He met the magistrate alone in Centennial Park at a time when the magistrate was dealing with criminal charges against his client Cessna, and also Milner. Further, he invited his client Cessna to witness the meeting.

2. Farquhar also had conversations with Ryan on the telephone. He asserted that he did not know on 15 May 1979 that the Cessna–Milner matters were to

be allocated to him for hearing. However, it is clear that it was his intention to deal with the charges to finality himself, at least from the time of the meeting in the park with Ryan. On any reasonable assessment, a magistrate acting bona fide, would not have dealt with the charges summarily, in view of the amount of the drug involved.

Members of the task force interviewed witnesses who had given evidence to the Royal Commission. Most had lapses of memory. They could not, or would not, remember any worthwhile evidence, even though it may have been given at the Royal Commission.

Little progress was being made by the task force until August 1986, when I was contacted by the Australian Federal Police, informing me that they had received information from their liaison officer in Thailand concerning the whereabouts of Timothy Milner. He had been the victim of an abduction and assault and was hospitalised in Bangkok. He could, perhaps, provide evidence to support what was now only suspicion.

INTERVIEW WITH MILNER

I flew to Thailand, where I met with members of the American Drug Law Enforcement Authority and the Thailand Narcotics Control Board. Inquiries revealed that Milner, now 50 years of age, was a long-term resident of Thailand.

Several weeks prior to my arrival, Milner had been kidnapped by two German nationals and held hostage for nine days. A demand of $750,000 was made by the captors to Milner's 'business' partner in Thailand to ensure his release. While in their custody, the Germans strapped a golf ball in Milner's mouth and assaulted him with a cricket bat, attempting to gain knowledge which would enable them to infiltrate Milner's drug empire, which he and others had established. An operation had been mounted by the Thailand Police, resulting in Milner's release and the arrest of the two offenders.

I asked the Thai authorities for permission to speak to both Germans, but I was informed that they were being held in solitary confinement and any conversation had with me would 'break their solitude'. Enough said.

During his captivity, Milner provided his abductors with a 37-page handwritten statement detailing his past and present drug activities and the names of his associates. The American and Thai authorities were continuing their inquiries into those revelations.

From his written confession it became apparent that, prior to Milner's arrest in Sydney 1979, he had been very active as a drug dealer. Upon his release from prison in Sydney after the expiration of the non-parole period and his deportation to England, he had quickly resumed his illicit dealings in the supply and distribution of drugs.

A section of Milner's statement was of particular interest as it referred to the importation of marijuana to Australia from Thailand and his and Raymond Cessna's subsequent arrest in Sydney.

...1975 sailed to Australia with 50,000 sticks (buddha). Received approx. $50,000. 1976 sailed to Australia with

100,000 sticks. Received approximately $120,000. 1977 sailed to Australia with 150,000 sticks. Received approximately $300,000. 1978 sailed to Australia with 250,000 sticks but could not sell because of poor quality. After 1½ months was caught by police. Went to jail for 18 months but was paroled after eight months.

Then, further:

Cessna and I got caught by the police and I went to jail. In the meantime Cessna arranged bail money for me of $20,000. I stayed on bail for two months until my case came up. I was told by Cessna that if I paid money things would be easier. He would say a figure and then a different one ranging from $70 to $50,000. I went to court and was sentenced to 18 months, then when I was inside my lawyer visited me and I signed a letter for an unlisted $30,000. I knew it was to do with my case but did not know who was being paid. They also took my bail money also other money I had. I had about $1000 cash when I was deported in Jan '80.

The statement also set out the method of each importation of buddha sticks to Australia. A yacht, commanded by Milner, was used as the transporter. The illegal cargo was contained in steel chests and was carried from Thailand to Bernier Island, a small landmass off the coast of Carnarvon, in Western Australia. The trunks were buried on the island before the yacht proceeded on to port and underwent customs inquiries at Carnarvon. Milner would return to Thailand and later travel back to Australia by aircraft.

Together with Cessna, he would travel by four-wheel drive to Carnarvan, then sail in a small inflatable boat to Bernier Island to retrieve the buried drugs. The two men would then return to Sydney or to wherever their pre-arranged customers were located.

On 5 September 1986, I interviewed Timothy Milner in the office of the Narcotics Control Board in Bangkok. I spoke to him about his handwritten statement.

'Yes. That was belted out of me by the Germans that you sent. I was tortured and kidnapped,' he said. 'That's what this is all over, because of getting caught in Sydney. They lost money. Then you arrive.'

Milner was under the impression that the Sydney 'connection' had been responsible for his present predicament. He was assured that this was not the case. He agreed that although his lengthy statement had been forced out of him, it was true. He reaffirmed that he paid $50,000 to his solicitor, plus his bail money of $20,000.

…but obviously it got us the result. We played up the low drug content. That was the idea. I know it got mentioned in the news, but really that's all I know about it—the drugs we got caught with were only half of the consignment. We sold the first half for $300,000.

The true position as written by Milner in his statement was that he and Cessna could be considered to be major drug dealers on an international scale. This contrasted to the defence scenario created at the time of their arrests that they were two casual acquaintances, each helping the other to transport a quantity of worthless drugs from one location to another.

A portion of the submission made in court by solicitor Bruce Miles to Magistrate Farquhar and recorded on the deposition read:

> *These defendants appear to be the victims of their own addiction. They bought material which turned out to be very under the amount suggested. The goods they bought from the instructions I have, drug wise, are just about totally valueless.*

Timothy Milner was invited to return to Australia and give evidence on oath as to the contents of his statement. He declined. The possibility of taking criminal action against him and applying for his extradition was impossible, as no extradition treaty existed between the two countries. Timothy Milner was happy to take his chances in Thailand.

THE LEGAL DECISION

Evidence obtained by the task force was forwarded to the Office of the Solicitor for Public Prosecutions for consideration of what action, if any, could be taken against Cessna, Milner and persons associated with their court case.

On 17 February 1987, Solicitor General Keith Mason advised the Attorney General that there was not available admissible evidence sufficient to sustain prosecution against any persons involved with the Cessna–Milner case. Milner would be required to give evidence before a court in Sydney for his statement to be accepted.

Following his retirement from the bench, Murray Farquhar did 'return to the lion's den to retrieve his hat'. In

1985 he was found guilty of attempting to influence a magistrate in his determination of a criminal case. He was jailed for four years.

Farquhar was released from prison after serving 10 months of that sentence, but again he tested his luck. He was charged with possession of stolen property after being found in possession of paintings stolen from the Melbourne home of high-profile millionaire Samuel Smorgon, but was subsequently found not guilty of the offence by a jury.

In 1990, Farquhar again went back to 'the den' when he was charged over a conspiracy to obtain false passports for people he had recruited to steal gold bullion from the Philippines. This time, the lion pounced. On 3 December 1993, during his trial at the Sydney District Court, Farquhar suffered a heart attack and died a short time later in hospital.

Whatever had been Murray Farquhar's motive for dealing with the Cessna–Milner court case in the manner in which he did would remain speculation. He took that answer to the grave.

CHAPTER SIXTEEN
THE JOB

The NSW Police Force is affectionately known as 'The Job'. Not only in New South Wales, but interstate and internationally. Wherever I travelled throughout the world, if someone said they were 'in the job', I knew immediately that I was in the company of a fellow police officer.

Knowing police officers as I do, each has one main objective when they join the job—to help. That desire may be achieved in many ways—arresting an offender, rescuing a crime victim, saving an accident casualty, quelling domestic violence, crowd control, traffic control, delivering babies, crime solving and security escorts are some that come to mind.

The police officer sees more sunrises than most people, takes a deep breath before delivering a death message to a grieving relative, sees other people's children more often than his own and puts his life on the line every time he leaves his home. He is always there when needed.

There are those, however, who are forever critical. If the officer lives in a brick home or owns a motor car, they will say, 'He's on the take'. If he lives in a fibro house, the line will be, 'Who's he kidding?' If he associates socially with fellow officers, then 'He's part of the police culture'.

Sometimes an officer's actions may result in the award of a medal. Other times, the officer's relatives are the recipient of the award, posthumously. But the greatest reward that can be given is a handshake and the words, 'Thanks mate.'

Such a thank you came in the form of a letter to one of my officers who had been involved in an accidental police shooting:

> *Dear Sergeant,*
>
> *I know that I speak for the majority of thinking Australians when I thank you for your dedication to your incredibly difficult and risky job. Have no doubt, Australia is fortunate to have you and your fellow officers.*
>
> *You must sometimes despair of the way the Australian media can distort the truth and make out that an act of incredible courage (which I know you simply believe is part of your job) is just a sensational story that will maximise newspaper profits. But remember that the Australian media is not the Australian public.*
>
> *Never forget that the alternatives to what happened would most likely have been the deaths of many innocent people. Don't change your attitude, don't become cynical. The lives you save will never be reported for they don't make news.*
>
> *Fortunately, you and the other members of your group have the guts to take extraordinary personal risks for the wellbeing of the community. Fortunately, your families give you the support that allows you to do this important work.*
>
> *I admire you all, for you are the reason that this country is*

so much safer to live in than most of our Western counter-
parts. To my mind you are all undoubtedly heroes, in the
same spirit of the Anzacs who fought to keep this fantastic
country free from tyranny.

I dips my lid to you, your fellow officers and your families.
Yours sincerely,
Dick Smith

IN THE LINE OF DUTY

The investigation of crime does not come without a down-side to policing—a fatality to a police officer. Whether at the end of an offender's weapon or by personal trauma, the result, unfortunately, is the same.

On 24 April 1989, Constable Allan Wayne McQueen was murdered in Sydney. His death is recorded in the chapter entitled 'Young Courage'. Shortly after investigating that murder, I completed my tour of duty in the NSW Police Force and retired. There have been too many police killed on duty to include in this book. I chose the ten-year period following my retirement to show the continuing danger to police. To bring the record completely up to date, I have added officers James Affleck, Glenn McEnallay and Christopher Thornton.

Sergeant Hobson

Sergeant Warren Patrick Hobson was a 40-year-old officer attached to Campsie Police Station in southwestern Sydney. On 17 March 1989, he was riding his bicycle to work when he was involved in a tragic accident in Croydon Park. He was admitted to Royal Prince Alfred Hospital suffering from brain damage and quadriplegia. These injuries resulted in his death from complications after pneumonia, several months later.

Sergeant Hobson had been awarded the National Medal on 8 June 1988.

Constable Allan Wayne McQueen

Constable McQueen was 26 years old and attached to the Sydney Police District Anti-Theft Squad. He had been a police officer for two years. About 11.30am on Monday 24 April 1989, he was part of a three-man team patrolling in Haig Street, Wolloomooloo, looking for suspected car thieves. He was knocked to the ground and shot twice when he asked a possible offender for his identification.

McQueen was conveyed to Sydney Hospital in a serious condition. He fought for life until 5 May 1989, when he died from his wounds.

Constable First Class Figtree and Senior Constable Rampling

On 13 June 1989, Constable Peter Allan Figtree, who was attached to the Ballina Highway Patrol in the north of New South Wales, died as a result of multiple injuries he received in a motor accident while he was in pursuit of a stolen car. The observer (and passenger) in the police vehicle was Senior Constable Glenn Donald Rampling, also of Ballina.

As the police car drew abreast of the stolen car south of Wardell, the offenders drove their vehicle into the police car, forcing it into a telegraph pole. Constable Figtree died instantly and Rampling died later that day in Lismore Base Hospital. The police officers were 25 years and 31 years old, respectively.

The Job

Senior Constable Eastes

Senior Constable Grant Charles Eastes of the Lismore District Accident Investigation Squad took his own life with an overdose of a prescribed medication at Chermside, in Queensland, on 13 January 1990. The officer was suffering from acute post-traumatic stress disorder at the time of his death.

At 5am on 20 October 1989, one of Australia's most horrific motor vehicle collisions occurred on the Pacific Highway near Grafton in the state's north. An inter-city express passenger bus and a semitrailer were involved. Twenty people were killed and a further 23 were injured. Constable Eastes was recalled to duty from his home and attended the scene of the accident. His duties included the extraction of the badly mutilated bodies, among them children, from the wreckage and 'labelling' them for identification.

The police officer had to psychologically cope with the massive trauma, chaos and magnitude of the collision during his investigation, which continued well into the following night. He became involved with the survivors and their relatives as well as relatives of the deceased persons. One survivor lost six members of his family. Three months later, Constable Eastes took his own life.

Constable Short

Twenty-eight-year-old Constable Kenneth John Short was attached to Engadine Police Station in the south of Sydney. On 11 July 1990, Ken responded to an armed hold-up alarm at a bank in nearby Jannali. The police car in which he was a passenger was involved in an accident and Ken was killed instantly. He had been a police officer for five years.

Detective Constable First Class Oakley

Detective Constable David Ian Oakley was 26 years old and stationed at Wagga Wagga in southwest New South Wales. On 18 December 1988, during the arrest of an offender, he was kicked in the face. He sustained loosened teeth and facial lacerations, and bruising and swelling to his face and jaw. The officer underwent surgery, but a malignant melanoma developed. Detective Oakley returned to work during 1989 and early 1990. However, on 14 August 1990, he died as a result of the injuries he received in his earlier attack.

David Oakley had been the recipient of a Police Commissioner's Commendation for his display of leadership during a riot at the Bathurst Motor Cycle Races in 1985.

Senior Constable Tickle

Senior Constable Peter Tickle was 36 years old when, in December 1990, he took his own life with his service revolver while in a distressed state at his home. The police officer had been attached to the Tactical Reponse Group and, five weeks earlier, had been involved with a police exhibition at a community fete held at Castle Hill Public School, northwest of Sydney.

The media severely criticised police for allegedly allowing children to handle police weaponry. The media reports weighed heavily on the officer's mind and there was a marked change in his behaviour. Despite assistance and support given to him by his fellow officers, the trauma became too much. Peter Tickle had been a police officer for 12 years.

Detective Senior Constable Whittacker

Thirty-one-year-old Richard Charles Whittacker was a detective senior constable attached to the Gosford Drug Unit on the state's central coast. He was involved in a major drug investigation which resulted in the arrest of 18 offenders who were charged with a total of 75 offences.

Three of the principal offenders made allegations that they had paid money to the police to drop the charges. Detective Whittacker was investigated by the authorities and exonerated. When the offenders were convicted and appeared in the Sydney District Court for sentence, the presiding judge vindicated Whittacker and other police and commended them all for their dedication to duty.

Detective Whittacker died on 28 September 1991 as a result of a cerebral haemorrhage. The report of specialist medical advice suggested his death was due to the pressures the case had placed on him. The officer received a posthumous promotion to the rank of detective sergeant.

Detective Constable First Class McNamara

On 20 October 1991, 24-year-old Detective Constable Bradley Bernard McNamara, attached to the North West Region Crime Squad, collapsed from heat exhaustion while training at the NSW Police Academy in Goulburn. He was conveyed to Goulburn Base Hospital and later transferred to the Prince of Wales Hospital in Sydney. While receiving intensive care treatment, Constable McNamara passed away on 31 October 1991. His death was found to be due to renal failure following heat exhaustion.

Constable First Class Hernandez

Juan Carlos Hernandez was a qualified weapons instructor and a member of the State Protection Group. On 30 November 1992 he received a gunshot wound to his upper chest during training at the Redfern Police Complex. Hernandez underwent emergency surgery at St Vincent's Hospital, but failed to recover. He died at 2pm the same day.

Constable Hernandez joined the NSW Police Force on 18 February 1987 and served at Waverley, Rose Bay and in the Operations Unit of the elite State Protection Group. He was 33 years old.

Sergeant Proops

Sergeant John Sidney Proops was a 43-year-old police officer attached to Enfield Police Station in Sydney's inner west. On 22 May 1993, the sergeant attended a house at Enfield in response to a call from a woman regarding a breach of a domestic violence order. A struggle took place between the officer and the offender and both fell to the floor.

The sergeant suffered a heart attack and all efforts to revive him at the scene and later at the hospital failed, and he died shortly afterwards. He had been a member of the force for 23 years and had served in the operations field at a number of inner-city stations.

Senior Constable Tidyman

At 2.30pm on Monday 15 August 1994, Senior Constable Dallas Leonard Tidyman, 37 years old, was fatally injured in a motor vehicle accident on the Lachlan Valley Way in Booroowa. He was riding at the rear of a column of six cyclists when he was struck by an oncoming vehicle. At the time he was acting as an instructor for the School of Traffic and Mobile Policing at the NSW Police Academy. His funeral was the first to be held in the NSW Police Chapel at the Police Academy in Goulburn.

Detective Senior Constable Nugter

On 17 March 1995, 34-year-old Detective Senior Constable Jack Alexander Nugter was driving a police vehicle on the Gilgai Road near Inverell. The rear wheels of the vehicle left the carriageway, onto the loose gravel shoulder of the road. The detective lost control of the vehicle and it struck a tree. He was fatally injured in the impact.

Detective Constable McGrath

Detective Constable Peter James McGrath had been a police officer for eight years when, in August 1992, he attended an armed robbery taking place at the Apia Social Club in Sydney. He arrested the offenders at great personal risk to himself. Then, in November of the same year, he was brutally assaulted in Sydney's Kings Cross district.

Two years later, in 1994, Detective McGrath investigated a horrifying case of child abuse. The detective suffered work-related post-traumatic stress disorder, followed by deepened depression. He was placed on sick report.

On 15 June 1995, 32–year-old Peter McGrath fell to his death from the seventh floor of a block of units in Glebe. He was married with two young children.

Senior Sergeant George

On 8 June 1995, 37-year-old Senior Sergeant Wayne Raymond George, attached to the School of Traffic and

Mobile Policing at the Police Academy in Goulburn, was riding a police motorcycle on the Picton Road on his way to Sydney. He was thrown to the road when his motorcycle was struck by a car, and three other vehicles, including a semitrailer, ran over him.

Senior Constables Addison and Spears

At 12.35am on 9 July 1995, an emergency call was received at Kempsey Police Station in relation to a complaint of malicious damage. Senior constables Peter Addison and Robert Bruce Spears, both aged 36 years, attended the premises at nearby Crescent Head. As they alighted from the police car, both officers were shot dead by a man armed with a high-powered rifle. The murderer then turned the weapon on himself.

Constable Carty

Twenty-six-year-old Constable David Andrew Carty was stationed at Fairfield in Sydney's west. He had been in the job for three years.

On 18 April 1997, after completing an afternoon shift, he accompanied other off-duty police officers to the Cambridge Tavern at Fairfield. After a few social drinks, David Carty left the tavern, and was confronted by a gang of troublemakers as he approached his car. The offenders were aware David Carty was a police officer as he had spoken to some of them the previous day concerning their behaviour. He was punched to the ground, kicked, stabbed in the heart and nose, and had one ear severed in the attack. He died almost instantly.

Senior Sergeant Smith

Senior Sergeant Raymond Keith Smith joined the NSW Police Force in 1970. He was 47 years old when, on 13 July 1998, he was killed in a tragic road accident. He was riding a police motorcycle on the F3 Freeway at Calga, north of Sydney, and was following a truck loaded with timber. A large piece of timber fell from the truck, striking the officer in the head. He was killed instantly. At the time of the accident, Sergeant Smith was attached to the Traffic Services Section at Parramatta.

Constable Forsyth

Constable Peter Forsyth was 29 years old, married with two young children. He joined the NSW Police Force in 1995 and lived with his family in the inner Sydney suburb of Ultimo.

On 27 February 1998, he was off duty and in the company of two other off-duty colleagues. When the officers were nearing Peter Forsyth's home, they were approached by several persons offering to sell them drugs. The three young police officers announced that they were policemen and a struggle took place as an arrest was attempted. During the altercation, Peter Forsyth and another officer were stabbed.

Constable Forsyth assisted his wounded mate, but he himself collapsed and was rushed to hospital. He died one hour later.

Detective Sergeant Dean

Detective Sergeant Leonard Graham Dean died of a heart attack on 29 May 1991. The attack came following long hours of duty investigating the murders committed by Paul Gerald Mason in the Queanbeyan Police District. The circumstances of the case are described in the chapter 'Friends'.

Senior Constable Affleck

Senior Constable James Affleck was attached to the Highway Patrol of the NSW Police Force and had been a police officer in excess of 20 years. On 14 January 2001, while on duty on the Hume Highway in Campbelltown, he was alerted by police radio to the approach of a speeding, stolen vehicle. The police officer ventured on foot onto the highway and laid a set of road spikes to stop the vehicle. The stolen car swung to avoid the spikes and struck the constable. Affleck died on impact.

Constable McEnallay

Constable Glenn Edward McEnallay joined the NSW Police Force in 1996, when he was 20 years old. At 6pm on 27 March 2002, while on duty as a member of the Highway Patrol section, he was alerted to a stolen car containing a number of young men in the Hillsdale area in Sydney's southeast. Constable McEnallay followed the vehicle into Grace Campbell Crescent, where it stopped. One of the offenders approached the constable, who was still seated in his car, and fired five shots. One bullet entered the constable's head and two struck him in the shoulders. The constable died of his wounds on 3 April.

Senior Constable Thornton

Senior Constable Christopher John Thornton was attached to the Highway Patrol at Gosford, on the central coast. He had been a police officer for 14 years. On the evening of 13 April 2002, the constable was in pursuit of a vehicle in Hillview Street, Woy Woy. The police car had the siren sounding and the flashing, warning lights were activated. A car travelling in the opposite direction made a right-hand turn in front of the police car, forcing it out of control and into a power pole. Constable Thornton was killed instantly.

On 26 August 1803, Constable Joseph Luker, a law enforcement officer attached to the Sydney Foot Police (a forerunner to the NSW Police Force), was killed while on duty in Sydney. Two hundred years have passed since his death, but the 'war on the streets' continues. So, too, do the deaths of police officers, killed in the course of their varying duties.